CU00925018

Jack Pringle was one of the outstanding escapers of World War II, and was one of only two officers to be awarded the Military Cross for his escape attempts.

Colditz Last Stop tells the story of these extraordinary attempts. The author describes his first escape from a train near Rome, dressed as a woman. Later, from the Medieval fortress of Gavi near Genoa, he makes the only successful escape in its 600 year history through an underground reservoir, only to be captured a week later on the Swiss frontier. On being moved to Germany after the Italian capitulation, he teams up with David Stirling founder of the SAS. Together, they scale the barbed wire of a Russian POW camp in Austria; fully clothed, they swim a river under machinegun fire from the banks; climb the Tyrol alps until nightfall; elude the tracker dogs set on their trail – and all of this in harsh mid-winter. Previously, in Calabria, Pringle had been suspected of being a spy, but had manage to evade the firing squad; later, with Stirling, he is given a suspended death sentence in Germany for the same reason.

When escape was not on the menu, the two were busy setting up subversive activities from within the prisons. While at Marisch Trubau near the Polish border, they made contact with the Czech Underground, and from within Colditz itself they worked with local German dissidents.

This is an amazing adventure story, the more so because it is true. In his laconic style Pringle makes no attempt to dramatize. But with the reality of a story covering four countries, eleven prisons and six escapes, there is no need to.

Major Jack Pringle, whose family have lived in Jamaica since the last century, attended school in New England before entering Sandhurst. Commissioned into the 8th Hussars in 1935, he was later posted away from his Regiment to command a squadron of Armoured Cars during the Abyssinian Campaign, where he was awarded the Military Cross. Returning to the 8th Hussars, he was captured in Libya in late 1941, and for the next three-and-a-half years he was either a prisoner or on the run. He was awarded a bar to the Military Cross for the escapes he made during this time.

Leaving the army after the war, he was engaged in business independently in Italy, Germany, Portugal and Africa until retiring to Wiltshire where he now lives relatively quietly with his wife. His lifetime interest has been in horses, and he now spends much of his time with them, but he has still found time to study at The Open University, and has recently gained a BA degree in History.

COLDITZ LAST STOP

Four Countries, Eleven Prisons, Six Escapes

Jack Pringle

Foreword by David Stirling

Temple House Books
Sussex, England

Temple House Books
is an imprint of
The Book Guild Ltd.

This book is sold subject to the condition that it shall not, by
way of trade or otherwise, be lent, re-sold, hired out, photo-
copied or held in any retrieval system or otherwise circulated
without the publisher's prior consent in any form of binding or
cover other than that in which this is published and without a
similar condition including this condition being imposed on the
subsequent purchaser.

The Book Guild Ltd.
25 High Street,
Lewes, Sussex

First published 1988 by William Kimber & Co. Ltd.
© Jack Pringle 1988

First paperback edition published 1995

Printed in Great Britain by
Athenæum Press Ltd.
Gateshead.

A catalogue record for this book is
available from the British Library

ISBN 1 85776 029 8

To Virginia

Contents

Foreword

by

Colonel David Stirling DSO

This book is different from most books about escape.

Jack Pringle's exploits cover six escapes as well as the setting up of an active liaison with the Czech Resistance and with German dissidents from within POW camps. His canvas is international, his wanderings carrying him through Italy, Austria, Germany and Czechoslovakia. He also holds the unique if questionable accolade, which I share with him, of having been a prisoner of war at both the designated 'punishment' prisons in Italy (Gavi), and Germany (Colditz). I found his description of the difference between the two to be especially interesting.

Jack himself had the right qualifications for the job. He had travelled in Europe before the war, spoke Italian, German and French, and had an adaptable character that allowed him to fit in whether in prison or out. He appeared to be just as much at home travelling in a crowded Italian train bound for the Swiss frontier as he was tramping with me through the Austrian Tyrol when trying to reach Jugoslavia, or when contacting the Czech Resistance in a church near Prague. Probably most important of all, as Alastair Cram and myself discovered, he was very steady when things became difficult.

He has a tendency to understate some of these difficulties and dangers that he encountered. For instance when he and Cram were escaping from Padula, their route was clearly more dangerous than he indicates. Passing by a sentry with a machine gun at thirty yards range in a floodlit courtyard was probably not as routine as he describes it.

His adaptability served him well, and was one of the reasons

9

why he never seemed to fret over being a prisoner of war. When not on the move he used his time. At Gavi he learnt German; at Brunswick he studied Buddhism; and during the last six months at Colditz he spent six hours a day reading Toynbee's formidable *A Study of History*. In fact he managed to combine the active with the thoughtful life to an unusual degree.

When I first met Jack fifty years ago, I knew him, amongst other activities, as a polo player who financed his chance to play by schooling polo ponies. Today fifty years later he exercises his mind by studying for his fourth Open University Course and stays physically fit by schooling polo ponies when he gets the chance – just as he did all those years ago.

For me, this book vividly revives memories of some exciting times together.

DAVID STIRLING

Prelude

It was January 1934 and I stood leaning on the railing of the *Bremen* as she steamed slowly into Southampton Water. It was an exciting moment for me as I was arriving from my home in New England and leaving my studies at Harvard University to enter Sandhurst. This was my first sight of England.

Although my family had lived in Jamaica since early in the last century, my father had left after the First War and gone to live in America. I went to school there and eventually to Harvard; but my ambition had always been to become a cavalry officer in the British Army as many of my family had been. Eventually, but not without avoiding some rules and regulations, I had been admitted to Sandhurst on the recommendation of the Governor-General of Canada; and I left the university after only a month. From an early age I had had a romantic concept of the British Empire, its history and all that pink on the map. Now I would be able to go and patrol it, or so I thought.

I arrived at Sandhurst that afternoon and was given a hideous suit of brown canvas and instructed to wear my civilian cap at all times, indoors and out, and to take it off whenever I saw an officer. New cadets were marched everywhere at great speed – 180 paces to the minute – by the company sergeant-major, the most important person in the life of a first term cadet. I was lucky, as the sergeant-major of my company, responsible for discipline and drill, was a model soldier. Coming from West Country yeoman stock, Sergeant-Major Pratt of the Grenadier Guards looked and was a real professional. Tall, spare with a blond moustache and blue eyes that were kind but could be frightening, he was exacting and fair. He took extra trouble with me, as, unlike the rest of my term, I knew nothing of drill or of military discipline, and he gave me private lessons in rifle drill in his company office. He was surprisingly solicitous of my feelings.

'Well done, Mr Pringle, sir,' he would say, 'but not at all what I want.' This after a failure to slope arms properly.

My great friend was Pat Hanbury, a person of charm with a good sense of humour. He took Sandhurst lightly, broke out of bounds regularly to go to nightclubs in London and, generally speaking, behaved like a civilian sentenced to spend eighteen months at a Military College. His escapades caused him to spend much of his time confined to barracks; but in spite of a distinctly unpromising start, this unruly cadet later commanded the King's Company of the Grenadier Guards – the very pinnacle of discipline – and became Lord Lieutenant of Bedfordshire.

He talked to me about London and introduced me to it, including some refinements. When we broke the rules to go there to nightclubs, we would get an ambulance to collect us in the early morning hours at our favourite nightclub, The Florida, and we would sleep on stretchers, arriving back at Sandhurst fully refreshed.

However, all this was yet to come, and for the time being I was on my own. Eventually, a promising opportunity was presented to me to sample this big world. It came in the form of an invitation from a friend of my father's to attend a fancy dress ball to be given at his house in Eaton Square. I applied for leave and was granted it, setting off in the Green Line bus one Saturday at 3 pm.

In the bus I planned what I would have to do. Obtaining a costume before the shops shut was the first thing. My friends advised me that if I went to the area of Covent Garden I would find shops that provided costumes for the theatre. After getting lost and wasting an hour I found just such an outfitter at about 5.30 pm. I approached the attendant.

'Have you got a costume that would fit me – something picturesque with gold braid and plumes?' I asked tentatively.

'Well,' he said, 'about the only thing your size are the

12

vegetable costumes from *Jack and the Bean Stalk*. There are carrots, peas, lettuce and potatoes.'

'Carrots,' I said. 'Give me a carrot.'

The carrots were too big. Peas and lettuce were too small. Only the potato suit fitted. This was a brown bombazine affair, tubular, with green sprouts fanning out around the collar where one's head came out. A brown cap with more green sprouts topped this vegetarian outfit. It would not present me in the dashing role I had planned for myself, but it was by now seven o'clock and I had no choice but to take it. I was pretty disappointed.

I was due for dinner before the ball at 8 pm. I wasted no time, and rushed out calling a taxi.

'Gorblimey!' the driver said. 'What are you supposed to be?'

'A potato,' I answered shortly. 'Three hundred, Eaton Square, please.' It was very difficult sitting in the taxi enveloped in my costume which was supported by wiring. I draped myself across the seat and could see the driver eyeing me suspiciously in the mirror. Getting money out of a pocket to pay the fare was a task for a contortionist.

At last I was ready and rang the bell of a very large house. It was clear I was the first.

A butler answered the door, and took a step back in surprise when he saw me, as everyone else had done.

'Good evening,' I said amicably. 'I am dining with Mr and Mrs Cottesmore.'

The butler took my box and advanced, leading me towards a high door. He turned to me.

'What shall I say?' he asked.

'Potato,' I said. 'I'm a potato.'

He opened the door and stood aside.

'Mr Potato,' he announced, closing the door.

An elderly man and his wife were at the far end of the room having a drink. They looked at me with courteous surprise. When I explained who I was they welcomed me but regretted that I had come on the wrong night. The ball was to be next week. I did not attend.

In spite of this failure to become involved in the life of a London season, I enjoyed my time at Sandhurst, losing some of my American accent as I tried to become British. I eventually became a cadet under-officer and could shout at others instead of being shouted at.

I passed out of Sandhurst and was commissioned into the 8th King's Royal Irish Hussars. As they were stationed in Cairo, I had, according to the rules, to spend six months with a regiment in the UK. So, in due course, I reported to the Scots Greys in Edinburgh with two Sandhurst friends, Hugh Brassey and Alastair MacDuff, and spent these months with them before going out to Egypt by troopship to join my own regiment.

Cavalry regiments varied a lot in character. Some had the reputation of being too rich; others were considered to be rather dull; there were charming but inefficient regiments; there were those devoted to racing and others to polo. There were a few who tended to have factions amongst themselves.

The 8th Hussars could not really be categorized. I found that they were an attractive cross-section with a refreshing variety of interests, and, above all, a happy family, with no factions. From colonel down to the newest-joined subaltern there was an attitude of friendliness and loyalty. I joined with two others, Jack Comyn and Henry Huth, and we agreed we had been more than lucky in our choice.

We lived in what was called the Harem Barracks. Whether or not the officers' mess had really been a harem or not, it was certainly a very fine building in late nineteenth-century Turkish style with thick walls to keep out the heat. All the rooms were enormous with fine proportions. A carefully tended garden with exotic trees, shrubs and flowers surrounded the building, and was enclosed by a high wall covered in bougainvillaea.

Just after I joined, the regiment was mechanized along with the 7th and 11th Hussars who were in Cairo with us. Everyone hated the whole concept of mechanization, which was accepted with distaste. But we kept to our interests and had about sixty privately owned polo ponies between us. The old riding school staff of roughriding sergeant-major and NCOs were kept on to run the riding school and train our ponies. All subalterns had to attend riding school every day as before. In Cairo we did not work very hard. Subalterns were paid only eighteen shillings a day and so did not feel guilty at the rather sparse hours we worked, which were from 6 am to noon five days a week. Except for manoeuvres which took about two months a year, the rest of the time was ours to spend as we liked.

But training periods on the desert were taken very seriously, and the time we spent on manoeuvres was exacting and interesting. With our light cars we had great mobility, and our war games covered vast areas – from the Mediterranean to the Siwa Oasis and from Libya to the Canal. We became very familiar with this vast expanse of desert, so much so that after a while we were often able to dispense with maps and compasses by recognizing familiar features, and at night we could navigate by the stars. We became very professional; and it was well that we were, as the war of movement against Rommel's forces and the Italians was not far off.

Life in Cairo was extremely pleasant. There was polo three days a week; racing on Saturdays and Sundays; sailing and deep sea fishing two hours away; and probably the best duck shooting in the world. Although hot between May and September, the rest of the year had an ideal climate – cloudless skies, very dry, and a moderate temperature.

Even in those days Cairo was a big city of more than a million, rich in history and archaeological interest, and with a broad spectrum of nationalities. There was the indigenous Egyptian population, ranging from those living in squalor and poverty to the fabulously rich pashas, landowners, bankers and merchants. Then there were the Copts, Christian Egyptians, who filled the role that Jews did in other countries, running the banks and financial institutions and exerting much power behind the scenes in government.

Much of Cairo's cosmopolitan atmosphere derived from its large community of Greeks, French and Italians, not to mention the British Cavalry and Guards Regiments and the large Diplomatic Corps. All these groups entertained lavishly, and young officers could, if they liked, dine out most nights of the week. Then in February and March, London debutantes of the previous season would come out with their chaperones, and young subalterns were in great demand.

It was not long, however, before this pleasant and hedonistic life was to end. The regiment was ordered to Palestine.

This was 1936, the year in which the Arabs started to protest in a militant way against Jewish colonization of Palestine as provided for under the Balfour Declaration. The Arabs were not really organized. Their resistance consisted mainly in aimlessly firing at British troops from ambush as they went about their duties, and in attacking Jewish settlements at night. Occasionally they tried to blow up the railway. It was a good-humoured kind of war.

After six months in Palestine the regiment returned to Cairo, where it had been stationed since 1934. These years, right up to the outbreak of war, saw Mussolini at his most bombastic. Abyssinia had been invaded and taken over. Now Nice, Corsica, Tripoli and Albania were threatened. These threats were shouted over the radio periodically to assure the Italian people that Mussolini was a fighting man – 'a lion', in his own words.

And, although we led a very pleasant life in Cairo, whenever the Italians became bellicose, we would be ordered out to the Western Desert in case of an attack on Egypt from Libya, which belonged to Italy. In April 1939, they suddenly and without warning walked into Albania.

At the time, I happened to be on local leave staying at Luxor as a guest of Barbara Hutton who was entertaining a house party on a boat anchored on the Nile outside the Winter Palace Hotel. She loved Egypt and had come out every year since her divorce from Count Kurt Reventlow.

It had been a fascinating week, as she had hired the chief archaeologist of the Cairo Museum to be available to explain to her guests the wonder of Luxor and Thebes. One evening a bearer arrived from the hotel with a telegram for me. It was from my Commanding Officer and said, 'Report to the regiment forthwith.' I boarded the Cairo train that night, and joined up with the regiment just as they were leaving barracks to cross the desert to Mersa Matruh, that desolate encampment that we knew too well from past scares. Here we were destined to spend the next two months.

However, in a few months time the emergency was over for the time being and we returned to Cairo. I found that my finances were not in good shape, that my polo ponies would have to be sold, and that the wisest course for me would be to join one of the Colonial Forces on secondment for a few years. Here pay was double; but more important, most stations were fairly remote, offering little temptation to spend money – very unlike the many opportunities that Cairo offered.

And so I said goodbye temporarily to the 8th Hussars and prepared for a brief exile in Nigeria where I had been posted to the 2nd Nigeria Regiment of the Royal West African Frontier Force. On 1st September 1939, I boarded a Nile steamer in Cairo en route to Khartoum whence I was to fly across Africa to Kano.

Then, as I sat in a deckchair watching the peaceful scenery on the banks of the Nile slip by, the radio announced that England was at war with Germany. My first thought was that I was trapped going in the wrong direction and that I would miss the war – very bad luck for a regular officer with some military ambition. The war was bound to be fought in Europe – or so I thought – while I languished in an outpost isolated and immobilized.

My destination, Kano, was the most important province of Northern Nigeria and comprised the area north of the juncture of the Niger and Benue Rivers. The people were Hausas, comprising the old empires of Bornu and Sokoto. They were a huge Muslim group with a cattle-raising and agrarian economy. Kano had, for centuries, been the greatest trading post between Senegal and the Sudan; and it was the stopping place for all pilgrims travelling east across the Sahara on the way to Mecca. Hausas and a smaller people, the Fulanis, were at the centre of this great movement of trade, and together were the ablest and shrewdest traders in Africa.

Kano was a romantic city, among African cities at that time third in population only to Cairo and Omdurman. It was encircled by walls about thirty feet high and twenty feet wide, made of burnt mud, and they completely encircled the town. The span of twenty feet on top was used as a road, arrived at by ramps every quarter of a mile both inside and out. The Hausa men wore voluminous white robes, carried spears and went about mounted on pony stallions. It was a spectacular sight to see these men galloping along the top of the wall, and using the ramps to descend into the city at the required place, in much the same way as we use spaghetti highways today. They rode at top pace, brandishing their spears.

The centre of the city was the palace of the Emir of Kano, the most important ruler in that part of North Nigeria. Several hundred thousand people lived inside the walls and there was a huge market place. It was possible in this market to buy almost anything: leather goods, hashish, horses, jewellery – these were only a few of the hundreds of different things on sale. It was infinitely more interesting and varied than the bazaars of Cairo, Tangiers or Marakesh, and I spent hours wandering around it during my six months' posting there.

The 2nd Battalion of the Nigeria Regiment, RWAFF, occupied barracks about two miles outside the city. It was an élite force of black troops under British officers. The men – all six feet tall or more – were recruited from many northern tribes. There were men from Bornu, Katsina, Sokoto, Maidugari, Yola, and many other provinces. Rather like the Gurkhas, these men considered it an honour to be accepted as a soldier in the RWAFF and soldiering was often a family tradition. There was a long waiting list, and only those with high intelligence and a fine physique were accepted. One of the attractions for them was the colourful uniform they wore except when actually in the field. This consisted of a green fez, a scarlet waistcoat buttoning to the neck with yellow braided frogging and a scarlet cumberbund underneath; khaki shorts; with bare feet and legs, oiled so as to shine. Like most Africans, they had a fine, soldierly carriage, and their drill was not inferior to the Brigade of Guards. Discipline was extremely strict and they were troops you could be proud of.

I soon settled into this new life which mainly consisted of

training, but which left time for polo twice a week and the occasional country race meeting. The north was a country abounding with horses – ponies of little more than fifteen hands that were a mixture of Barb and Arab. I had half a dozen to play polo on, each costing about £10. In the late afternoon, I would ride out into the countryside with my groom as guide, talking with the natives to improve my Hausa. Before dinner I sat on the veranda of my bungalow studying Italian from a set of Linguaphone records. It looked to me pretty certain that Italy would come into the war, and I reckoned that it might be useful to know the language.

I was right on both counts: Italy declared war on England immediately after Dunkirk; and, because of my Italian, I was posted to the Nigerian Brigade Headquarters as Intelligence Officer.

Almost immediately the brigade embarked for East Africa. There were half a million Colonial and Italian troops in Eritrea, Abyssinia and Somaliland, and both Kenya and the Sudan were threatened by this huge force. Neither of these countries had garrisons remotely approaching the strength of the Italians, probably two brigades each at the time of Dunkirk, with long frontiers to defend.

The Nigerian Brigade disembarked at Mombasa, but almost immediately I left them. Trained as I had been with armoured vehicles, I was quite sensibly posted to the East African Armoured Car Regiment. This was a most unusual outfit.

Most Kenya settlers of military age, when the war began, went as officers to the King's African Rifles, which consisted of East African black troops in the same way as the West African Frontier Force consisted of black troops from that area. But some Kenya settlers had different ideas. They wanted to form an all-white armoured car regiment in which they would provide all ranks up to troop leaders. Each squadron would be commanded by a regular British officer with another regular officer as second-in-command.

They got their way and formed the East African Armoured Car Regiment. I was posted as the second-in-command to a squadron commanded by Duncan Geddes, a Cameron Highlander, who had lost an arm in Palestine while winning an MC. I had known him there. He was a delightful man, not much older than myself, and a very good soldier. Unfortunately he was wounded shortly after I joined the regiment and so, during the Abyssinian campaign, I commanded the squadron.

I say that the regiment was unusual because of the characters that made it up. As is well known, in the twenties and thirties some people of spirit left England to settle in Kenya. They were fugitives from orthodox life and they went to make their homes in a beautiful country abounding in wild life, where they could farm, do nothing, or do anything they liked without criticism. They were often eccentric and all were independent-minded.

I was twenty-five when I took over command of 'A' Squadron. I found that my squadron sergeant-major, George Llewellyn, had been my uncle's fag at Harrow. He had been an alcoholic; but when war was declared he gave it up for the duration. I could not have gotten on without him. He had a commanding personality, understood the rather exotic troops that formed the squadron, and ensured loyalty in my first days of command. The squadron quartermaster-sergeant was a man of about fifty, head of the Kenya Legislative Council. One troop leader was a white hunter. Another was a charming remittance man. The third troop leader had been a major in the previous world war and had an MC and the Croix de Guerre. Among the other ranks were all sorts of adventurous characters, including RSM Duffield who had been a regular officer but had shot his commanding officer when he discovered that he was having an affair with his wife. He had served his sentence and at the start of the war was working on a Uganda newspaper. Everyone was from five to twenty-five years older than I was. I learnt that among themselves they called me 'the Boy'.

In February 1941 two divisions from Kenya – mixed East, West and South African – advanced into Somaliland and Abyssinia to take the Italians out of the war. A similar force moved in from the Sudan. My squadron was independently attached to the 12th Division, and we were the only armoured troops that General Godwin Austen, commanding the division, had available. The rest of the regiment was with the 11th Division and went into Abyssinia by a different route from us.

Then followed three months when my squadron had the task of leading the division's advance first into Somaliland across the Juba river, then back into Southern Abyssinia and finally up the Rift Valley north to Addis Ababa. During this time, and over a distance of nearly 2,000 miles, we always had first contact with the enemy. We had skirmishes with the retreating Italians and their colonial troops, but only one set-piece battle, during which I lost a third of the squadron killed or wounded. This was at a place called Uadarra where Mussolini was supposed to have used gas when taking over the country in 1936.

It is almost impossible to describe the wild remoteness of Southern and Central Abyssinia. It was in those days, and I suspect is even today, inhabited by people who owed allegiance to nobody.

There was one road, more like a track, that ran north and south. On either side of the Rift Valley down which the road ran were high purple mountains rising to 10,000 feet. Tribes lived in the re-entrants to these mountains who had never recognized the Emperor Haile Selassie, much less the Italians or the English. Access to the fastnesses in which they lived was difficult and pointless. These people had lived there from time immemorial and had practically no contact with the government which the Emperor claimed to control. In fact he ruled effectively for only about 200 miles each side of the railway from Eritrea to Addis Ababa and from Addis Ababa to Berbera, in what was then British Somaliland. I suspect that the present government of Ethiopia effectively controls little more than that.

By September 1941 the campaign was over, The Italians had been defeated, and my squadron was doing routine patrol work in the Danaquil country north of Dire Dawa.

One day a signal arrived: I could choose one of two alternatives:

21

either to go as second-in-command of the newly formed Southern Rhodesian Armoured Car Regiment, or return to the 8th Hussars in Egypt. Of course, I chose the latter. I had held the rank of major whilst commanding my squadron of armoured cars. Now I would revert to captain.

In early October I joined my regiment in Egypt, five miles short of the wire on the Libyan frontier. Armoured forces were massed there for an attack planned to relieve Tobruk, an attack which was launched on November 18 on a three corps front (although there was in fact no such thing as a 'front' in desert warfare).

My command during the advance into Libya was to be the 'Thinskins'. Thinskins only existed in times of action. They comprised about twenty vehicles carrying water, oil and petrol; their task was to stay close to the armoured squadrons of the regiment when on the move or in action, ready to replenish them when necessary. We had no armoured protection of any kind. I travelled in an open wireless truck.

Four days of almost constant fighting against Rommel's Afrika Korps brought the regiment to the heights above the Sidi Rezegh landing ground just south of Tobruk, where a tremendous battle had been going on for two days. The 8th Hussars had suffered severe casualties against the greatly superior tanks of the Germans, and had been brought into brigade reserve. My commanding officer, Dick Cripps, had gone at dusk on that 22nd of November to Brigade H.Q. to reconnoitre the battlefield from a ridge that ran along the edge of the airfield, and I accompanied him, leaving the Thinskins about three miles away. We had a good view of the battle which was still going on. All was dust, smoke and confusion. Burning tanks, aeroplanes and vehicles of all kind littered the landscape. There was no front in the orthodox sense of the word, and we could see wounded men staggering around uncertain which direction to go in. Just before dark the enemy put down a smoke screen, launched a strong attack, and by 5 pm were in full possession of the airfield.

Almost at once our Regimental Headquarters came under fire

from anti-tank guns which, under cover of smoke, had moved close up, and could fire over open sights. Headquarters and one squadron retreated and I followed them. From my open truck I could see gun flashes and tracer all around me. When out of range, we halted and formed a close leaguer. In order to bring in the rest of Brigade Headquarters Very lights were fired and soon we heard tanks approaching. These, we thought, would be tanks of the brigade and everyone dismounted to show the newcomers their place in the leaguer. I was about to drive out and find my Thinskins when a group of tanks drove into the leaguer and we heard German being shouted from the tank turrets. It was a detachment of the Afrika Korps.

Fighting at close quarters between tanks and men on the ground broke out. Climbing into my truck I made a run for it, leaving the dogfight behind. I set off due south to find the Thinskins, but after travelling for about ten minutes I could hear movement of vehicles all around me – impossible to tell whether friend or foe. I decided to leave my car and walk, as I would be able to lie down if vehicles approached and wait to see who it was.

After walking for fifteen minutes I heard vehicles approaching and I lay down in some scrub in a shallow wadi. Suddenly a spotlight shone on to me and a German tank rolled up, letting off a burst of machine-gun fire over my head. I got slowly to my feet and put my hands up.

Three days later with other prisoners taken during the fighting around Tobruk, I arrived in Benghazi and was put into a barbed wire compound guarded by Italians. It had apparently been agreed that all prisoners taken by the Germans would be handed over to the Italians, and we were pleased about this. Shocked and disappointed as we were, we nevertheless thought of prison life in Italy as being comfortable; lots of spaghetti and chianti, with idle, inefficient guards. In fact no one had the slightest idea of what prison life would be like. For my part I looked forward to an early escape, and, using my Italian, a rapid trip to Switzerland and home. This proved to be very far from what was actually to happen to me in the next years.

CHAPTER ONE

Mont Albo, Rezzanello, Rome

After two days about ten of us, seemingly selected at random, were suddenly warned that we would be leaving our Benghazi prisoner of war camp within the hour. We paraded, and were marched down to the port where, much to our concern, we were embarked in a submarine. Concern arose from the fact that our navy was active and very effective in seeking out and sinking submarines.

However, we were given our first good meal for six days by the sailors who seemed friendly, and I immediately went to sleep on the deck, not waking up until we put into Taranto, Italy's southernmost naval base, the next morning. We were greeted by an officer of the Carabinieri (Royalist Police) in a splendid blue cloak. I took charge of our party as I spoke Italian. Yes, I said to the Carabinieri, we would very much like breakfast. I presumed we would have it at the police station. Not at all; we were loaded into a truck and taken to one of Lloyd Triestino's most modern cruise ships, lying idle at anchor.

The dining room was empty, but a table had been laid for us with silver cutlery and linen table cloths. We had four waiters looking after us, supervised by a maître d'hôtel. Breakfast was orange juice, coffee, bread, smoked ham, cheese and red wine! We ate ravenously – as much as we liked – and the red wine bottles went round and round. We all agreed that the service was excellent, but of course we expected this from Italian waiters.

We felt replete and most amiably disposed to our captors. If this was the form, we felt we could easily adjust ourselves to life as prisoners of war in Italy. Probably they would take us to see some of the great galleries and sights of Italy. They were, after all, a civilized nation, as clearly witnessed by our reception. Feeling a sense of rapport with these apparently friendly people, I asked for cigars for my companions and these were immediately produced – good Cuban ones, not ones made from Abyssinian tobacco as we had expected.

The Carabiniere officer came up to me and saluted respectfully 'The transport is ready to take you to your transit camp,' he said.

We got off the ship and into an open lorry; six guards accompanied us. We were cold, as we only had the clothes we had been captured in, and became colder as the driver put his foot down on the accelerator and coaxed the lorry into maximum speed. One of the guards told me we were going to Brindisi – about thirty miles away.

By the time we arrived, we were frozen; shirtsleeves being the wrong kit for an Italian winter with a flurry of snow. But we felt sure that when we arrived we would be given coats – perhaps leather, lined in sheepskin from the Abbruzzi? Also there would be another fine meal. So there was lots to look forward to.

The lorry drew up outside two high rows of barbed wire, and we dismounted. The gates opened, there were sentries in towers either side, and we were faced with an elderly Italian lieutenant, a sergeant and a few soldiers. The lieutenant was the interpreter. Barbed wire extended in a square of about 300 yards on each side. There were more sentry towers at each corner and sentries were on patrol outside the wire. Six lines of wooden huts were all there was to see, and the country around was flat, bleak and uninteresting.

'Your barrack is the one on the right,' explained the interpreter. 'Go in and wait. You are the first here.'

The sergeant and his men accompanied us to the door which he unlocked.

'*Ecco*' he said. 'There you are.' They departed.

We entered. There were twenty iron cots on each side of the hut with about two feet between each one and a corridor of eight feet running between the rows. On each bed was a burlap mattress irregularly stuffed with straw.

'What the hell!' I exclaimed to my companions. 'This can't be where we are supposed to stay?'

I was wrong. We were indeed to stay there, and in place of the sheepskin coat I had looked forward to receiving, we were each given one thin blanket. I asked when we were going to have a meal, and was told 'later'. I tried to go out and see the lieutenant but there was a guard on the door. It got dark, and there was no light. We sat on our cots very hungry, as we had had nothing to eat or drink since morning. At last the lieutenant appeared. With him were two soldiers carrying a big dixie and a corporal holding ten tin bowls and ten spoons, which he gave us.

'*Mangiare*,' said the lieutenant.

The corporal dished out one spoonful of spaghetti to each of us and one piece of bread. Having done this, he and his men withdrew leaving a sentry with a candle at the door where a bucket had been left as a convenience.

The early fantasies of life in Italy as a prisoner were over. No more smoked ham for breakfast, no more chianti. Exhausted, I covered myself with my blanket and went to sleep. Realization of what POW life would be like now started to get through to me.

*

The word 'prisoner' conjures up thoughts of confinement and immobility, and usually it does indeed mean that. But in my case it turned out that during the time I was a guest of the Italians and the Germans, I was to lodge in no less than eleven prisons. I started at Brindisi in Southern Italy, and was successively sent to Lombardy, Basilicata, Liguria, and then to Austria, Berlin, Bavaria, Moravia, Hanover and finally to Colditz in Saxony. That is about 3,000 miles of travel, and I added another 1,000 miles while on the run.

Being moved around resulted from being a nuisance, or from having escaped. As a rule, after an escape a prisoner did not go back to the same prison if recaptured. Commandants tended to get rid of trouble-makers. Baiting guards, disturbing camp routine, escaping – these occupations made you unpopular and caused moves. I was definitely moveable.

The mentality of a prisoner and of the escaper is perhaps worth looking at.

Theoretically it is the duty of officers to try to escape, either to get back into action or anyway to occupy enemy troops required for guard duty – troops that otherwise could be used operationally. In fact there were any number of prisoners – by far the majority and among them very brave men – who simply felt that they would be lost mentally and physically if they found themselves alone in enemy country on the run. Few prisoners had experience of Europe; fewer still spoke Italian or German. Such men sensibly decided to sit tight and see the war out. Then there were the married men who, with equal justification, felt that taking the risk of getting shot during an escape was simply not the responsible act of a family man. I counted myself lucky in that I had no family responsibilities of any kind.

Those who decided to keep their heads down in prison life usually developed routines to make the time pass. They studied a language or some practical academic subject; or they fixed on a routine to alleviate boredom. They cooked for their mess, stood guard for escapers who were at work, raked leaves, or walked a fixed number of times around the compound every day. There were many unimportant tasks to which you could attach your life if you wanted to – small parochial errands. The passage of time could be numbed in this way.

Reading became important, and I have often thought how sterile the lives must have been for Japanese prisoners, who had no books. In Germany, and to some extent in Italy, prison camps had libraries made up from the books sent from England to relatives in prison camps and in most camps we had German or Italian newspapers every day. Colditz, perhaps the oldest of all prisons – 1940 – had an excellent library with books on such practical subjects as law, accounting, farming and shorthand. For the academically minded there were books on history, philosophy, economics, comparative religion. Some long-time prisoners passed law or accountancy examinations. Prisoners did not read novels as a rule. The life, oddly enough, was not conducive to romantic or adventurous thoughts. It was as if the mill of the mind, deprived of real-life experience, required academic material to grind.

The opportunity of being able to read widely and with a concentration rarely possible in the hurly burly of normal life was the most valuable benefit I got from those years. When a prisoner sat down with his book, he did not have to think of earning his living, dealing with family problems, or anything else. He may not have liked this isolation, but it was, in fact, a gift exceedingly rare in the outside world.

Of course there were those whose ideas were different. Bridge players, poker players, chess players – these spent most of every day at their games, every day for years. Very large sums of money were often wagered and lost, but at the end of the war not many debts were paid.

The escaper was a different animal and there were various types. There was the occasional man who simply could not stand confinement, the man for whom the attainment of freedom became an obsession. Mike Sinclair at Colditz, probably the greatest escaper of all, was such a one, and after many attempts he was eventually shot and killed during his final attempt at the very end of the war. Then there were those who devoted themselves to working on complicated escape routes – often tunnels which called for organizing, improvising and ingenuity. Usually those who went in for this type of escape liked the work involved, and the planning of what to do when free occupied their days and absorbed their thoughts. For many who became involved in such projects – projects which often took many months – the day-to-day work leading to a break was what they liked most. Being on the run in enemy country called for a kind of fox-like cunning and a great deal of luck. Nine out of ten escapers stayed out only a few days before recapture, and not more than a few dozen British prisoners ever made the 'home-run'.*

For myself, during the various times I was out, I found the

---

* Although after the Italian capitulation many did.

excitement of trying to evade capture quite without equal. The enemy hold all the cards. It was really a losing game, but I did not think of it like that.

*

The Brindisi camp filled up gradually, but life was pretty spartan, and there were no books nor anything to do. But one day that December of 1941, the Japanese attacked Pearl Harbor. America entered the war, and we all knew that in the end we would win. Before that, sober thought had made us wonder if it was possible. Oddly enough even when the Americans did come in, we all correctly reckoned the war would last another three to four years. There was no thought of early victory, and there was no doubt in anyone's mind that we would be prisoners for a long time.

Sometime just before Christmas we were put on a civilian train, and shipped north up the Adriatic coast. It turned out that we were going to a new prison, a palazzo called Mont Albo, not far from Piacenza. Mont Albo was a rotunda, the circular building having a courtyard in the middle which was our only exercise space. Like many small palaces built in the seventeenth and eighteenth centuries, there were no corridors, every room leading direct into the next. I was put into a room with ten others, and from the window next to my bed on the distant horizon I could see north across the plains of Lombardy where the Alps were visible on clear days, snow glittering in the sun.

I found friends there who had been captured in the same battle. One of them was John de Bendern, from the County of London Yeomanry, who had been British amateur golf champion. His father had chosen to leave England and now lived in Liechtenstein in great style. John had the idea of writing to him and asking him to send a driver down into Italy with a car load of chocolate and treacle. (We thought of nothing but these sweet things, I suppose because our bodies lacked energy from being short of real nourishment.) This was considered to be an excellent idea, and a letter-card was duly sent off by John.

For the next month we spent hours looking out the window at the road that wound up to the castle, expecting daily to see this car arrive full of sweets. The car did not arrive; but a brief note did arrive for John from his father. The letter said, 'Dear John, I am surprised that you have the temerity to ask such a favour. You have surrendered to the enemy, which is a disgrace. Yours – ' John's tank had, in fact, had a direct hit from a German Mark IV and he was lucky to be alive. Anyway, it was clear from then on that chocolate was off the menu; we were back to a small ration of spaghetti.

I bought some oil paints from the Italians and began a mural on the walls of my dormitory depicting hunting scenes. In this I was partnered by Mark Ogilvie Grant of the Scots Guards, a naturalist and botanist who had been captured during the Greek campaign. I painted the horses and Mark painted the landscape background. It was a freezing cold winter and we had no heat of any kind so this served to take my mind off the cold and kept me standing up. Many officers simply stayed in bed all day fully dressed, getting up only for meals. I was lucky also in being asked to act as interpreter for the Senior British Officer (SBO) and once a week I would go with him under escort down the hill to the Commandanture. I welcomed these little trips as it gave me a chance to reconnoitre the immediate surroundings of the castle in case I could escape, which by now I was planning to do – but without a solution as to how.

These meetings usually dealt with welfare. The Senior British Officer would discuss such all-important matters as food, clothing, books, medical requirements and discipline. The Commandant had his own interpreter. I was there to pick up what was said between them in their own language and to intervene in case the Italian interpreter (an ex-waiter at the Savoy) did not convey an accurate meaning. The SBO had insisted on this, and it was the only prison I was in where this arrangement was agreed to.

The Commandant was a poppycock of a man, highly scented and full of mannerisms easily imitated. He was also highly excitable, and capable of achieving a high-pitched squeal when giving his decision, for instance, on quantities of spaghetti to be issued to the cooks. 'No more! Not one! Nothing! Nothing at all!

Absolutely no more!' he would shriek, rising to his feet on the cue 'Absolutely'. I insisted on translating it all. 'No more, not one,' etc., and the SBO and I would smile and perhaps laugh as I drew out the translation.

This was a pleasant relief from boredom but it did not endear me to the Italian authorities, who hated being imitated or laughed at. So it was with little surprise that after about six weeks I was warned to get ready within the hour to move. I was told by the interpreter – quite a good fellow – that the Commandant considered that I translated with a bias hostile to my captors. This did not hurt my feelings.

An hour's trip in a Fiat with two guards brought me to another small and very pretty palazzo, Rezzanello – by strange chance originally the home of one of the Buccleuch family who had emigrated to Italy, had Latinized their surname, and were called Scotti. It was built on three sides of a cobbled courtyard, the building, I should guess, being mid-eighteenth century. It had been a prison for a year, holding about eighty officers, mostly captured at Mechili, and was my first taste of life where routines had been established, and where there was order and organization. It was in fact the best and most civilized prison in which I was ever to lodge, although exceedingly well guarded and with none of the architectural quirks which sometimes provided an escape route to the enterprising prisoner. In fact no one had managed even to attempt an escape during the year it had existed. But a fine view from the hill on which it was situated across a pretty valley to higher hills inspired the imagination with thoughts of freedom. I walked all over the castle and around the small strip of garden fenced with wire and covered by the usual machine-gun towers, but I could see no chance.

In any case, four months after my arrival, we were warned that we were all to be ready to move in two days' time. Clothing sent from families in England, books, Red Cross parcels – all these had to be packed, and we were told we would be travelling 'south' for twenty-four hours. We assumed that if the trip was to take twenty-four hours it would be to Calabria or anyway somewhere south of Naples. A long train trip set me to thinking how I could escape en route.

I decided I would get together clothes that would enable me to pose as a woman, and jump train. I had several yards of dark blue material that I had bought from a naval officer due for repatriation. This would do for a wrap-around skirt. The small Italian shop in the prison where a few odds and ends were sold kept a line in coloured handkerchiefs, and I bought the most vivid and largest one I could find. This would cover my head as a scarf. A light blue RAF shirt would do as a blouse. I got hold of a small tube of crimson oil paint to improve my lips, and I shaved off my moustache.

To carry out my plan I had to have accomplices who would travel in the same compartment with me and who would create a diversion. Four volunteered. Before we marched off to the station I crammed my disguise into the front of my battle dress. Myself and my four accomplices all managed to get into the same compartment. I had a seat by the window opposite a guard. Another guard sat next to the door leading to the corridor, prisoners in between.

The plan was that at a suitable moment during the journey two of my friends would start quarrelling over food, leading to an exchange of blows, while two others would try to keep them apart. Dealing with this situation would, I hoped, occupy the guards for a few moments, time enough for me to jump from the window.

I learnt from the guard that we would be passing through Rome, and as the Vatican was known to harbour escaped prisoners, it was my intention to make my bid when we got somewhere near. There were two things that would decide the moment. One was the speed of the train: we were travelling at about sixty miles an hour, and I would have to wait (and hope) that it would slow down to around twenty miles an hour. I also hoped that this slowing down would coincide with our passing through country where there was some cover. There would be little time between my jump and the time when the train would be brought to a halt by guards pulling the alarm cord. This is where my disguise was to help me. I counted on changing into my woman's costume in under a minute, and had practised it many times in the few days before entraining.

We asked for the window to be left slightly open as it was late May and quite warm. The guard obliged; and so by reaching I was in a good position to pull it down all the way when the time came. By late afternoon we were, I judged, not far from Rome, and I got ready for the jump. I waited and waited, but the train rushed on at high speed. Finally, we started to slow down, I felt that pleasant excitement that I was later to experience on other occasions just before *it was going to happen*! I gave the word for my friends to start quarrelling, which they did. We were passing through tall cornfields which would provide good cover, and my main concern was to avoid jumping out into telephone poles which seemed to pass with the frequency of a picket fence.

Eventually our speed levelled off. I decided it was now or never, and I gave the signal for the quarrel to turn into a fight. As soon as the guards got up to intervene, I pulled down the window and jumped, landing heavily, but the embankment slope broke my fall and I rolled down onto the verge of a cornfield. I could hear the train's brakes screeching in response to the alarm, and I knew I had very little time before they would be back searching.

I ran into the cornfield and unbuttoned my battle dress top which I threw away. I hiked my trousers up over my knees, wound the blue material around me, fixing it with safety pins, tied the kerchief over my head and smeared a little crimson paint onto my lips. It was my plan to be bold and walk back towards the railway hoping this would be clear proof that I was not on the run. This I did, going out of the field in the direction of the shouts of the guards. As I left the field I could see them three hundred yards away spreading out on both sides of the track. I walked steadily towards them, and shouted at one of them '*che é successo?*' – what's happened? He ran on past me. '*Prigionero scappato*' – escaped prisoner, he said, but he paid no attention to me and went on past. Much encouraged, I walked on towards the halted train.

Then it happened. I had not been able to roll up my trousers, but had had to pull them up. Now one trouser leg started to slip down below my skirt. A keen-eyed guard spotted it, and it was all over. I was surrounded by screaming guards. One guard was cooler than the rest. He smiled at me and winked. '*Che bella ragazza,*' he said, 'What a pretty girl!' I had to be content with this small reward as they bundled me into the luggage van under a guard of four soldiers.

It had been an unlucky affair, because it turned out that we were only about ten miles from Rome and the Vatican. After the war I lived in Rome for a few years and the flat I rented had by great coincidence belonged to one Monsignor Hemming who with Monsignor O'Flaherty had been responsible for dealing with many escaping Allied prisoners during the war, smuggling them from St Peter's into the Vatican itself. I would dearly have liked to have met them on that day.

I travelled the rest of the journey with my four guards in the baggage van. I was disappointed; but I had never had very high hopes of success. So I set out to make the best of the situation which was to get as much information as I could from these guards about our destination, and to talk to them about the war. This I always did with guards wherever I was, as I had my own means of communicating with the War Office, and views of the ordinary soldier were of real interest, giving as they did a good indication of national morale.

It appeared that our destination was to be a monastery called Padula, fifty miles inland from Salerno. This was all they knew. As far as the war was concerned, they could not understand why they were in it. Why were they fighting alongside Germans? They had nothing in common with them. They didn't like them and the fact that Hitler and Mussolini were friends surely did not mean that the Italian people had to be friends with the Germans? The English were better people – gentlemen, in their opinion. This was a point of view that I heard over and over again during the next year right up to the Italian capitulation in September 1943.

The train halted for the night in Rome, but we were locked in the baggage van so there was nothing to do: no windows to look out – I went to sleep on the floor. At about four in the morning we started to move again. The guards – by now quite friendly – kept me informed of our whereabouts. Now we were in Naples. This was Salerno. We were climbing mountains, and so on. Finally the train halted, an officer opened the door, and I got out to join the others.

CHAPTER TWO

Padula Monastery, Basilicata

We appeared to be in a fertile valley with high hills to the south and east. We marched along a small country road, stared at by farmers driving bullock carts, and followed by an enthusiastic pack of little children. After half an hour's walk we saw our destination, a huge sprawling monastery set in the middle of about fifty acres of fields all contained behind a perimeter of fifteen-foot walls.

We entered a courtyard with a machine-gun tower in the centre, and were greeted by a smiling priest, one Father Volpi, who spoke good English and was the camp interpreter (also the camp black marketeer as it turned out). He wore a flowing black cassock, cross in place around his neck, and his manner was friendly. He addressed us:

'Welcome to Certosa di Padula,' he said, in the manner of a good hotel manager. 'You will be treated well here as long as you do not try to escape. There is nowhere for you to go. Please remember that.'

Big iron gates swung open and we entered the monastery. Going first through various corridors with rooms on either side that were obviously offices, guardrooms and the like, we finally arrived at massive double doors which were closed. Keys were produced and many locks unlocked. Then we were searched as was usual whenever entering or leaving a prison, but it was a negligent search, and all maps, knives and compasses got through. We were clearly in the hands of people with little experience of guarding prisoners, or of prison discipline. It was in fact a new prison recently opened to accommodate prisoners

37

taken during the running battles in Libya and Egypt that had been going on during the first six months of 1942. Officers and guards all appeared to be learners in the art of keeping prisoners confined, and this was a good omen.

Padula was vast, said to have the largest cloisters of any monastery in Europe. They were arranged in a square, about 150 yards on each side, supported by Ionic pillars. Off the cloisters were what obviously had been the monks' cells, now rooms for officers above the rank of lieutenant. Each room held eight officers, and there was one window in each room facing out onto barbed wire about six feet away. Guards patrolled the wire inside and out, and there were the usual machine-gun posts at regular intervals. There were no guard dogs. Outside the wire were fields of grain, some grazing-fields as well, and then the fifteen-foot-high wall that, as far as we could see, went right round the whole complex.

Running overhead above the rooms where I lodged and above the cloisters was the original ambulatory for the monks. There 400 lieutenants lived in one huge corridor of a dormitory running around all four sides of the building – two feet between beds and six feet to the wall, where windows overlooked the interior courtyard.

As the prison (*Campo di Concentramento* as the Italians called it) had only been open for about two months, organization was chaotic. Food, cooking facilities, plumbing, systems of roll calls, issue of letter cards – all problems to do with these things were dealt with in utmost confusion, if dealt with at all. But there were advantages. As I could see, the lay-out of the monastery was irregular and had many unpredictable architectural features making it very difficult for the Italians to guard it effectively. It took the Germans nearly five years to make Colditz escape-proof, but here at Padula there was what one could, with certainty, call virgin territory. This gave me the feeling for the first time since I had been a prisoner that there was a real chance of escape.

I started seriously to think about it. The very location inspired my imagination with ideas of freedom. We were in a beautiful, valley – we had glimpsed its richness as we marched to the monastery from the train. Fields of corn, grazing cattle, vegetable gardens, small irrigation canals, and leisurely peasants at work in the fields made me feel quite close to real freedom. The mediaeval atmosphere of confinement in the monastery itself – uncomfortable and chaotically run though it was – seemed somehow acceptable for the moment. Most tantalizing was our view of Padula village perched high on the side of a rocky hill only about half a mile away. Like so many villages throughout Italy, it had been built there because fertile land such as lay in the valley was so precious that no one wanted to waste one square metre of the soil by putting down a house on it.

We could see from the monastery the day-to-day life of the villagers. Women put out washing from the windows of their pink houses; men drove sheep through narrow lanes down the hill between the houses; children ran riot around the small village square, set at an angle on the hill. Sometimes a young girl would stand and wave at the monastery anonymously. Prisoners looking out of their windows would wave back, although of course we could not be seen. I could not wait to get out into this friendly-appearing countryside.

For my escape I wanted a serious partner. By now I had been inside long enough to know that the idea of escaping provided a constant source of conversation and was fascinating for practically everyone. But very few of the talkers were really serious, and fewer still applied themselves to the task of figuring out how to do it.

I circulated around the monastery and talked to the prisoners who had been there for the two previous months. I wanted to find someone who had actually made an escape before getting to Padula – that is, someone who had performed. I found him: he was Alastair Cram, a gunner lieutenant, captured, like myself, at Sidi Rezegh.

Cram was known throughout Padula for having escaped and having remained at large in Sicily for some time before being re-captured. He was not difficult to identity as every morning at dawn, in a corner of the cloisters, he stripped to the buff and carried out fifteen minutes of the Mueller exercises, a strange

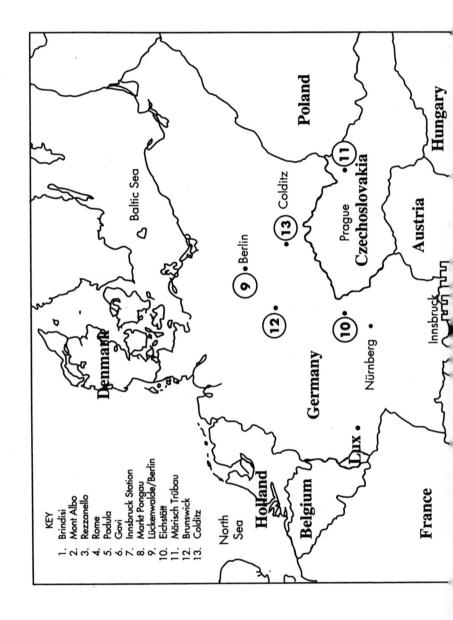

KEY

1. Brindisi
2. Mont Albo
3. Rezzanello
4. Rome
5. Padula
6. Gavi
7. Innsbruck Station
8. Markt Pongau
9. Lückenwalde/Berlin
10. Eichstätt
11. Märisch Trübau
12. Brunswick
13. Colditz

North
Sea

Holland

Belgium

Lux •

France

Germany

Denmark

Baltic Sea

• Berlin

⑨

⑫ •

⑩ •

Nürnberg
•

Innsbruck

Poland

⑬ • Colditz

Prague
•
Czechoslovakia

⑪ •

Austria

Hungary

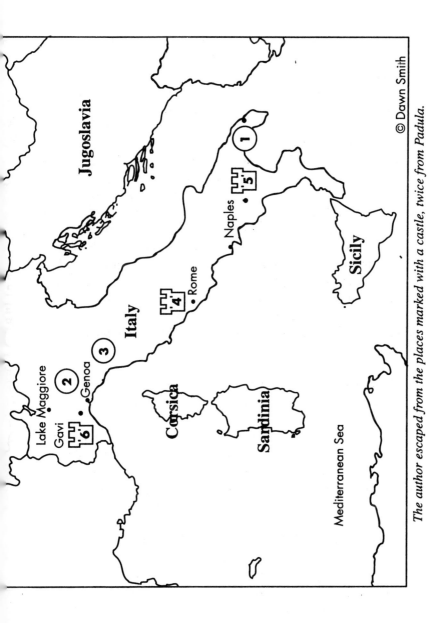

The author escaped from the places marked with a castle, twice from Padula.

© Dawn Smith

41

combination of manipulation of the limbs combined with massage. Nothing was allowed to interfere with this regime.

I went to talk to him. He was stocky, with a hawklike face, piercing blue eyes and fair, curly hair.

He was friendly but reserved. Many prisoners simply wanted to hear the story of his wanderings in Sicily; and, as I came to appreciate later, Alastair was too preoccupied with thoughts of escape to enjoy long rambling talks to no purpose. Someone with this fixation was exactly the person I was looking for, but first I had to convince him that I was serious. My attempted escape from the train gave me some credentials, but Alastair like myself was a loner and not inclined to team up with anyone. He was about five years older than me and in our talks I learnt quite a lot about him. Before joining up he had practised at the bar in Edinburgh but his real passion was mountaineering and he had climbed most of the difficult peaks of Europe. Much to my surprise I found that he spoke German and Italian, albeit with a good healthy Edinburgh accent. Eventually, not without a certain difficulty, I managed to convince him that reconnaissance of possible escape routes could best be done by partners. We became partners.

Following the idea shared by both of us, that the monastery was bound to have exits not yet spotted by the Italians, we began to go over the place yard by yard. We looked out of every window, tapped all walls, identified sewage systems, noted guard routine, kept watch on the fields surrounding the monastery so as to observe moves of the peasants who farmed them, and generally familiarized ourselves as well as we could with the movements of everyone we could see, and with the architectural lay-out. We talked to guards with the object of finding out what happened in the adjacent part of the buildings where the Italian guard company lived, and where all the administrative offices were. Gradually we built up our picture of the place, and we kept our knowledge strictly to ourselves.

But even before I teamed up with Alastair I had spotted a possible exit route, and now we made a plan together to try it out.

Padula Monastery, Basilicata

The plan involved getting out into a small courtyard from the monastery kitchen which was manned by our own soldier cooks. In this courtyard, two Italian masons, attended by a guard, were mending a wall. Every day they went off to their lunch by passing out through our kitchen into the administrative block. We intended to dress as nearly as possible like the masons, and to let ourselves out into the courtyard just before they were due to return. There was a different guard every day so we hoped he wouldn't notice us too closely and mark the differences in our appearance.

An escape is best done alone, and I think that we were each wondering how the other would behave. I needed have no fear. Alastair was absolutely steady, and we both began to enjoy ourselves as we hid up in the kitchen after the masons had gone off to lunch. But first a cook came up and looked at us.

'One moment,' he said. 'You're missing something.' He opened a cupboard and took out a bag of flour. 'Dust that on to yourselves. Masons' clothes are always covered with cement.' We did as he said, then we took a deep breath, opened the door and entered the courtyard.

The sentry was sitting with his back to the wall half asleep. His rifle was, reassuringly for us, on the ground on the other side of the enclosure. He opened one eye.

'We'll be working on the outside of the wall,' I told him. 'Give us a shout at five o'clock.'

'*Va bene,*' he replied – and he closed his eyes again. We climbed over the wall into an open field, reached the road and made for the village. No one was about. It was siesta time.

But our freedom was shortlived. We were each carrying a small bundle with some food, and as we passed through the village square these attracted the attention of two Carabinieri lounging in a doorway. They were always on the lookout for black marketeers.

'A moment!' one of them shouted across the square. We stopped. 'What are in the bundles? Open them.'

I suppose we should have run but we didn't. Inevitably the Carabinieri found our chocolate, coffee and cigarettes, all from the

43

Red Cross. It was clear that we were not black marketeers as they had suspected, but were from the monastery, and we were soon back in the office of the Commandant, who was furious and voluble. He gave us thirty days in the cooler.

Much to our surprise and satisfaction he did not confiscate our olive-green Greek trousers or our ragged sweaters, so that we remained clothed in our mason's outfits.

It proved to be a useful month. Our cell was just inside the only entrance to the monastery complex, that is to say, the entrance area where the guards lived and the administration took place. This area had to be passed through before the prison cloisters were reached. On the other side of the corridor from us was the guardroom door. Through the bars of our cell we were able to observe all movements of the Italian guard detachment and the guard-changing routine. We could also see everyone who entered or left the monastery by the one and only means of access – the main doorway close to our cell.

We noted every detail of these movements. One thing puzzled us however. We could not figure out what happened every two hours when a door nearly opposite was unlocked by the corporal of the guard who would disappear, coming back a few minutes later with two soldiers. The corporal would leave the two men in the guardroom and go away for about ten minutes, probably to make his report, leaving the door open. He would come back and then parade two other men from the guardroom, and march them in through the mysterious door. What was behind this door? What were guards doing in there?

Watching these comings and goings passed the time, and we were lavishly fed from our own kitchens. A batman brought us twice the normal ration three times a day, and a glass of marsala each as well. It was a little like being on board ship – meals marked the passage of time.

On the thirtieth day we were escorted through the administrative block and released into the cloister areas to rejoin the other prisoners.

Alastair and I now took stock of what we had learnt. There were two things. The first was that we had some knowledge of what went on in the administrative and guard company block which formed the area outside the cloisters. Our vantage point of the prison cell had given us a useful knowledge of the comings and goings of the guards and the administrative staff. Secondly we had been able to observe the lay-out of this area, sealed off as it otherwise was from the prisoners' complex within the cloisters. Our brief escape had whetted our appetite for another one, because it had really been a very simple exercise.

Alastair insisted that we always wore our Greek trousers and airforce blue shirt and that we carry our Italian lire on us. He said we should be instantly prepared to escape if we got a chance. I agreed, but I could not see this happening without a lot of preparation.

However, only a week after serving our thirty days' detention, we were walking around the cloisters at about two in the afternoon, a time when everyone took it easy on their bunks. It was June, fairly hot, and no one was about.

Suddenly we saw a ladder propped up against a wall quite near to the entrance between the administrative block and the prison cloisters. The top of the ladder rested against an open trap door about fifteen feet from the ground. Ladders always had guards with them. We looked around. No guard was in sight.

There was no need for words between us. We climbed the ladder and pulled it up behind us, closing the trap door silently. Instead of having to jump down into the room from a ledge, we found ourselves sitting on a pile of mattresses. What was below them we couldn't tell. It was pitch dark so we decided to stay quite still and wait until our eyes grew accustomed to the darkness. We also listened for noise coming from the cloisters. There was none.

After a while we were able, very dimly, to see where we were. Apparently we were in a room in the administrative block used to store mattresses. The room, to the height of seven feet, was full of mattresses, and we were sitting on top of them. There was no window and we could see nothing.

Our worry was, when would the owner of the ladder come back? When he found it gone, would he report it? Maybe not, as he would be in trouble, but sooner or later there would be a roll call followed by a search. We would have to make a plan at once if we were to take advantage of our situation.

We slid down off the mattresses and, feeling our way in the pitch dark against the wall with our hands, we came to a doorknob and a door.

We listened for a while but could only hear very faint voices somewhere in the distance. Finally I opened the door gradually and looked out onto a small courtyard.

It was closed on all four sides by the building, but there was a door halfway open to the right. Through it, we saw two guards sitting at a table chatting with their backs to the door, looking out of a window. It was evidently their voices we had heard. We watched them for ten minutes and they never moved. It was clearly their duty to watch the wire and fields outside.

Our predicament was now very real. In spite of our luck in getting out of the prison cloisters undetected, we were faced with a most discouraging situation as our only possible way out was blocked by these two armed guards in a room twenty feet away. There was no hope of using our ladder to climb out of the courtyard. The ladder was only ten feet long and the surrounding walls of the building were thirty feet high.

So we had to decide whether or not to try the only thing possible. This was to go through the guardroom carrying our ladder and to do this whilst the guards were actually in the room. The ladder would be a tremendous impediment to our movements, but it would be vital for scaling the walls if we succeeded in getting out. The prospect was daunting, not least of all because the guards, if suddenly frightened, might use their revolvers on us at very close quarters.

We sat on our mattresses discussing the chances. Alastair's legal training made him prudent and analytical. Would we throw a shadow when we entered the room? No, because the June sun was around the corner. When entering the room, would we cast a reflection on the window that the guards were facing? Again no, because the glass had no dark background. Where were we? The

46

more we thought about it the more convinced we were that the exit from this little room would lead to the door opposite our detention cell, close to the main entrance of the monastery itself.

We decided to have a go. We would try to pass through the room we could see, behind the two guards looking out of the window, leave by the exit we couldn't see, and then take things as they came. We would have to gamble on finding the corridor leading to the main entrance, and would make our attempt at the 8 pm guard change, when it was just about to get dark and a June haze would be settling in on the countryside.

All this had taken us to about 6 pm. We now had two hours to wait before making our attempt and we spent most of the time looking through a crack in the door, watching what went on in the guardroom. To a certain extent, what we saw was reassuring. The two men, on taking over, sat down immediately and never left their posts, staring steadily out of the window except for an occasional sortie out of our sight, which we assumed was to the lavatory. But time dragged and tension was high. At 7.45 pm we stood ready for the guard change. If we were to take advantage of the open door, we had to make our move five minutes after the relief that came on at 8 p.m.

On the hour, the corporal appeared and marched off with the old guard. Two new guards settled at the table.

Now we had to go. We were ready, our boots tied around our necks so that we would make no noise on the stone floor in our stockinged feet. I opened the door, and carrying the front of the ladder, moved out into the courtyard, so that Alastair, carrying the other end, could follow. The moment had now come to see if we could go through the room without disturbing the guards.

I walked slowly forward with my end of the ladder, and Alastair followed with his. As I entered the room I saw the exit door through which we would have to leave behind me to the left – thank God it was open. I inched forward until I was about six feet behind the guards. They were talking and looking steadily out of the window. By now, Alastair was just in the room with his end of the ladder. Suddenly, one of the guards pushed back his chair.

We froze, hearts in our mouths. If he got up, we were finished.

But no, he only wanted more room to put his elbows on the table. And so, after a moment's pause, I started the most perilous part of the exercise. I had to move to my left and backwards so that Alastair could move forward into the room and into the same position I had just left, that is, with the ladder six feet from the guards' heads. When he got to this position, I was then free to leave the room through the rear door and he to follow.

Unbelievable as it may seem, the manoeuvre was successful and the turning movement was carried out. The guards saw and heard nothing. Fortunately Italians are garrulous people and the guards had never stopped talking.

Leaving the room, I looked ahead down the corridor and – yes! the door opposite our detention cell was open.

In a few seconds we had passed through that door and were at the open entrance to the monastery complex, free to leave. It was getting dark. As we stood there peering out, the floodlights went on.

So far so good. But we knew from our observation whilst in the detention cell, that the yard, dominated by a sentry tower with a mounted machine gun, was walled in on all four sides with only one exit door which was always kept locked. This meant that we would have to cross the floodlit courtyard, clearly visible to the sentry in the tower, if he was looking, and we would have to do this carrying our ladder. We could not clear the wall without it.

It was not a good prospect, but having got this far there was no going back. Alastair looked around the corner. He whispered that the sentry must be on the far side and out of sight. He could hear him spitting. The machine gun was on a swivel facing us but momentarily unmanned. We had to hurry.

With our boots still tied around our necks, we crossed the yard making no noise, and leaned the ladder against the wall. The most dangerous part of the exercise would now take place. If we succeeded in getting to the top of the wall, we would be level with the sentry and staring into his machine gun thirty yards away and in full view under the floodlights.

Padula Monastery, Basilicata

The gods favoured us. We both made it safely to the top of the wall where a hasty glance revealed the sentry with his back to us gazing towards the village where lights were starting to go on one at a time. Quickly we pulled up the ladder, using it to clamber down the far side. Out of breath on the ground, we looked about us to see where we were.

If we thought that we were finished with walls, we were wrong. We found ourselves in a ten-acre field of barley entirely enclosed. A sprawling farmhouse and some barns ran along one side of the field far to our left, and the remaining three sides were bounded by high walls. We got to our feet and started for the wall opposite, still carrying our ladder. Progress was slow. The ripening barley was difficult to wade through. Then, when we were halfway across, a dog started to bark, near the farmhouse. We stumbled on as best we could, but the dog came rushing towards us. We heard a voice yelling at him to shut up. The dog arrived at the looming dark wall just as we did, barking more and more insistently. What was worse was the sight of a man standing in the light of the farmhouse door. We were pretty sure he couldn't see us but there was no time to lose. We used our ladder again and climbed over the final wall, hid it in a ditch and set off up the hill towards the village. We were free!

*

We knew where we would head for. We had, after all, walked right through the village of Padula before being recaptured after our previous abortive escape, and so we did the same thing again. There was no one about, not even a dog, and we were soon out of the village into the forest on the far, upland side.

We had no food, no false papers, nothing – but we did have quite a lot of Italian lire obtained by selling Red Cross chocolate to the guards. So once again we decided to go east towards the town of Potenza where we would try to find a train north to Milan and then to the Swiss border. There was no alternative to a train: it was around five hundred miles to Switzerland.

Alastair was an experienced climber, and we now had to leave the village and climb up through the woodlands on a steep narrow path. He told me to keep my knees slightly bent while climbing. This, he said, took a lot of the strain out of climbing. But he set off at such a pace that, bent knees or not, I had great trouble in keeping up with him. He rolled about in front of me like a small boat in a heavy sea, and scorned any idea of resting.

We climbed until mid-morning, when we saw in front of us a small hut in a clearing. Alastair reckoned it would be a woodman's hut, perhaps a charcoal burner. We approached it cautiously. It was unoccupied.

After the excitement of the escape and the strenuous haul up the hill we were exhausted. We decided that one of us would sleep and the other keep watch. We spent the day like this. In late afternoon while it was still light we started east again along a forest path which now started to descend into a valley over open country.

We set off down the hill towards a village we could see in the valley. It was a long way off, and we felt pretty secure. We had no intention of going into the village, but of skirting it and continuing over the hills still in the eastern direction towards Potenza.

Walking down the hill we saw in the distance that we were approaching a flock of sheep attended by a shepherd, a bearded man of about sixty dressed in corduroys, a checked shirt, neckerchief, and leaning on a staff. To avoid him would be suspicious, so we walked straight on.

Like all people who spend their time alone, as shepherds do, he watched us but said nothing. When we were a good way off I suggested to Alastair that we ask if there was a stream near by where we could find water. We were thirsty after the last twenty-four hours without water. Then I would have a reason to engage him in conversation. We wanted to know what lay ahead, as we had no map, and only knew very vaguely where we were. We were somewhat concerned with our appearance, and certainly looked a bit odd in our green knickerbockers, blue shirts and desert boots, but there was nothing we could do about it so we walked slowly towards him.

To explain my accent, I told the shepherd we were German deserters from a Panzer draft going south from Austria to join Rommel's army in North Africa. We had jumped train in Naples, and wanted to get back to Austria.

This struck a sympathetic chord. Having established the fact that we were Germans, I handed over to the blond, Nordic-looking Cram, and he carried on the conversation in his best Edinburgh-Italian.

It turned out that we were not far from a reservoir and a power station that had been attacked very recently in what must have been the first British parachute landing of the war (it was now July 1942). Although the attack had failed, it had alerted all the troops and police in the area. In other words, we were in a region where everyone – ordinary citizens as well as troops and the police – were alert and suspicious. This was bad news. Alastair asked what the locals thought of the Nazis.

'Enemies,' replied the shepherd, 'the same as the British parachutists.' This was, in fact, a pretty accurate view of what the average Italian thought of the Axis.

Our shepherd, now friendly, offered us some bread and cheese. We accepted because we were hungry and said we would like to pay. 'No,' he said, anyone deserting from the war was his friend. We very much hoped to meet more like him; said goodbye, and moved off down the valley.

That night we slept near the village in a vineyard concealed from sight. Before dawn we started east again, up another range of hills similar to the ones we had just passed. Once again we bent my knees as Alastair had advised. Once again he went up the hills and through the woods like a long dog, and I could barely keep up with him. But we made good progress, met no one, and by late afternoon were looking down onto another village. This one lay in a bottleneck between two hills through which we would have to pass.

By this time we had been walking for nearly two days without any food except the piece of bread the shepherd had given us, although we had found many streams from which to drink. Looking down we saw some cornfields and decided we would approach them at dusk, eat some corn and then navigate the village.

We got into the cornfield and ate some green corn. Villagers came and went quite near us but we were able to find a spot where we could see the general lay-out of houses and streets without being observed. The village itself had not more than thirty houses or shops, and we would have to go through it or make a day's detour. This would probably have been the prudent thing to do, but we decided against it, and to pass through the village at night.

After dark we heard the usual noises that villagers and their children make. Italians are night people – two-year-old children are kept up until midnight while their parents sit talking and drinking coffee or wine in the square. So it was well after one o'clock in the morning before everything was quiet.

We had scrutinized the village carefully from our hide in the cornfield. It was typical of all southern Italian hamlets, with small houses and shops two storeys high, pink and white, and a tangle of very narrow small streets barely wide enough for a bullock cart to pass. Between houses were vineyards with irrigation canals that ran criss-cross through them and along the streets. Indeed, it was like a maze, and we were pretty certain that we were in for a difficult passage.

The village was dark and the narrow streets were unlit as we cautiously entered one of the broader of them. It was divided down the middle by the main canal.

'Thank goodness there are no dogs,' I whispered to Alastair.

This had been our great fear. I spoke too soon, for at that moment a dog rushed out from a dark alleyway barking furiously in a piercing high staccato note.

The owner of the dog was quick to react, memories of the parachutists no doubt fresh in his mind. In no time he appeared at the door carrying a lamp and shouting at us to stop. We backed off from the dog and into the canal which ran down the centre of the road. There was no alternative but to wade, waist deep, along it with the dog barking at us from the bank. When it flowed around a sharp corner out of sight of our pursuer, we climbed out on the far side and ran flat out down a lane.

Padula Monastery, Basilicata

Now the whole village came alive; doors opened, lights went on and people were shouting all around us. At once, coming towards us at a trot, we saw six Blackshirts, Mussolini's élite Fascist troops, carrying rifles and bayonets at the ready. We were caught.

We were roughly manhandled along to the Fascist barracks, receiving a fairly good beating with rifles, fists and boots on the way. We looked dubiously at the wall where huge letters spelt out that '*Mussolini ha sempre ragione*', 'Mussolini is always right'.

At this point, things were starting to look a bit bleak. We would have had no worry had we not been a few miles from the parachute landing area. But here there was bound to be strong, hostile feeling, and we could by no means be sure that rules of the Geneva Convention would be observed.

Our fears were reinforced when we were marched into the office of the Blackshirt company commander who sat behind his desk wearing dark glasses. He was threateningly cool, which was a bad sign. When Italians shouted you usually could be sure that there would be a calm after the storm. This captain just sat and looked at us and said nothing. Eventually he spoke in English – quite good English.

'What are you doing here?' he asked. We told him our deserter story.

'That is a lie,' he said. 'You are spies and if you cannot identify yourselves I have authority right here in this office to have you shot. And where are your comrades?'

We had no comrades. We were just two Austrian deserters. We persisted with our story.

'Another lie,' he said. He turned to the sergeant. 'Parade six men behind the guardroom with loaded rifles,' he told him in Italian, 'and put these two spies against the wall and wait until I come out.'

We were marched out into a small courtyard and duly stood up against a wall opposite the six soldiers. They stood clicking the bolts of their rifles. There was clearly no future, indeed there was a possible past.

'I wish I were in Edinburgh,' Alastair remarked.

'I wish I was in Padula,' I replied more realistically.

The captain appeared. It was no good. We told him who we were, and asked him to telephone Padula for confirmation. We stood against the wall hoping he would get through on the line while the men disconcertingly continued clicking their rifle bolts.

Eventually he came back.

'*Sono prigionieri di guerra,*' he said to his men. 'Take them to the cell.'

We were taken to a cell about eight feet square with no window. The door slammed and we were alone in the dark. Hungry, tired and disappointed, we were in no mood for a rambling discussion of our plight. We lay down on the concrete floor and immediately went to sleep.

After about twelve hours in the darkness, the door was unlocked. There stood the good Father Volpi, smiling and friendly as always, with four Padula guards.

'You are naughty boys,' he said. 'You might have got shot.'

The Blackshirt sergeant glared at us as we were bundled into a ramshackle truck and driven the thirty miles over winding mountain roads back to Padula. There we were put into the cell we knew well, the cell from which we had been able to reconnoitre the escape route we had taken just three nights before.

Clothes were sent to us from inside. We were allowed to wash. A generous meal was sent out to us from the cookhouse. We lay down and went to sleep again.

When we woke up we found the Commandant at the foot of our cots with his interpreter.

'You are a danger to the state,' he intoned. 'I am arranging for you to be sent to the punishment prison where you will live in cells cut into the rock, and be in chains. You will regret what you have done.'

If what he said was true we probably would regret it. But the idea of a move appealed to us both, and there was always the chance of escaping from the train. We were not at all depressed.

Next day a sergeant and four guards appeared with Father Volpi, who brought with him our few belongings – uniform and a Red Cross parcel.

'I am sorry, but you are to be handcuffed during the trip.'

Handcuffs were produced and we were marched out to the same ramshackle truck and driven with four guards to the local station.

On the way to the station Father Volpi told us that we were foolish to want to escape. After all, the war would soon be over. Morale, both in the services and among the civilians, was low and Mussolini's regime was increasingly unpopular.

'*Pazienza,*' he counselled.

I sent a report with these views back to the War Office in due course, by writing to my father. This I did through a code I had arranged with him before I went off to war in August 1939. I used it throughout hostilities and it turned out to be extremely useful, as a family letter couched in innocuous terms, was quite unsuspect. My father knew which letters were coded as they began 'Dear Father', whereas I called him 'Dad'. In the 'Dear Father' letters, he took the first letter of every other word. These, when put together, spelt out the message.

The train trip was uneventful. Handcuffed, and with four guards for the two of us, escape was out of the question. We had a long wait in Rome, and then during the night the train travelled north along the coast. It was bright moonlight, and we stayed awake to watch the small fishing boats at sea and the fields where flocks of goats and sheep fed. I felt a wave of nostalgia. The last time I had travelled this route had been on my way back from Egypt to stay with my old friend Pat Hanbury, whose family had a beautiful estate near San Remo with world-famous gardens. I had come down in the world.

We passed through Genoa, and by looking at the sun could see we were still going north. The guards had up to now refused to say what our destination was to be. Now they told us that we were getting out at a station called Aquata Scrivia, just north of the Ligurian mountains; and in due course we passed through the tunnel under the mountains and emerged on the plain on the other side. Within minutes the train stopped.

55

CHAPTER THREE

Gavi Fortress, Liguria – Part One

At the station we were handed over to a sour-looking lieutenant, and four Carabinieri. These latter prided themselves on being royalists, owing allegiance to the King and not to Mussolini. For this reason they were preferable as guards, because, although more efficient, they were usually more friendly, and, what was more important, ready to talk. They told us that the Commandant was a Carabiniere general, of which there were very few, and that there were twelve officers and 300 guards for one hundred and eighty prisoners. A depressing bit of information followed; no one had escaped in its six-hundred-year history, and we were to be confined in cells in the rock face. So he said.

Alastair and I were sitting outside in the back of the truck, and we had a good chance to look around us as we drove towards our destination – Gavi fortress. We soon could see it, a vast needle of rock rising high above the plain with the village of Gavi at its base. We drove through its tiny square where the locals looked at us curiously. I suppose the men inside the vast fortress were unreal to them, but Alastair and I were real, and deserved a thorough scrutiny. We waved at them with our handcuffs. The girls waved back, but not the men. I think Alastair's flaxen hair was the attraction.

'Forget it,' said a guard. 'Not for you.' As if we didn't know.

Now, as the truck started up the hill into the fortress we became alert. We knew that once inside we would not have another chance to see what the fortress was like outside. And so we looked at every wall, every sentry box, every wire complex, and at the outside structure of the fortress so that, if we ever had a chance to get out, we would have some idea of what we would encounter.

Gavi fortress (*Campo di Concentramento No 5*), close to the site of the battle of Marengo, was indeed a remarkable and forbidding place, and rather difficult to describe. It had in feudal days been a strong point against barbarians from the north. Its defence had been organized in three tiers, so that the defendants when attacked could retreat upwards from one fortified level to the next. We could see all this from the square. The jagged walls, bastions and turrets on three levels looked like a gigantic wedding cake made of stone.

The truck drove a short way up the hill and stopped at the base of the fortress. There we were told to dismount, and a huge iron door in the rockface opened. We were marched into the gloom.

Alastair and I both knew our Dante. 'Abandon hope all ye that enter here,' we said in unison, and we half believed it.

Proceeding down a dank tunnel paved with uneven stones we eventually came out into a small open yard with rock walls on all four sides. The tunnel door clanged shut behind us, and our handcuffs were taken off.

We were taken into a cell cut into the opposite side of this rock wall and given the only really thorough search I ever had during my years as prisoner. Seams in our clothing were slit to see if we had concealed maps. Toothpaste was squeezed. Heels of our boots were removed in case they secreted gold coins. No orifice was left unexplored. This took a full hour. Eventually the officer appeared to be satisfied.

'*Va bene,*' he said. '*Andiamo.*'

An iron-grilled door opened and we proceeded on an upward slope inside another tunnel, this time spacious and vaulted, arriving after a hundred yards at yet another iron grille, through which we could see prisoners lounging about in a walled-in courtyard or playing netball.

We entered. All the prisoners stopped whatever they were doing to have a look at the newcomers, and many greetings were exchanged with acquaintances from previous camps – all here for the same reason.

An officer in naval uniform came up to us.

'I'm Peter Medd,' he said, and, turning to the Italian lieutenant, 'I will show them where to go, Aldini, they'll be all right.'

He led the way to the end of the courtyard.

'I won't say "welcome" because this is not a very welcoming place, as you can see.' He was right.

We were in a rectangular cobbled courtyard about fifty yards by thirty. Cliffs up to sixty feet high rose above us on three sides. Against the back section of rock was a row of five large cells clearly constructed centuries ago. Forming the fourth side, and closing the rectangle, was a stone building built on two floors. Its outside windows looked south over Gavi village to the Ligurian hills. On this lower, courtyard level of the outside building were the batmen's quarters and the kitchen. An outside flight of stairs led up to the dining room, long and narrow, running the length of the building over the kitchen and over the batmen's quarters. Although the outside of this building had windows looking out on the world, we as officers lived in semi-gloom in the five cave-like quarters on the inside. This was because officers were not to have access to the outside world.

This, then, was the lower compound, first line of defence for defenders of Gavi fortress for centuries past.

'There's another compound up above,' Peter Medd explained. 'We go up to it by a ramp.'

The ramp was cut into a side of the rock face in a sweeping arc, and ascended steeply, so steeply in fact that we were out of breath when we reached the top. It was closed from 8 pm to 8 am sealing off one compound from the other, was covered by a machine-gun turret high above, and patrolled by sentries.

We entered the top compound, virtually the same as the first, with three sides hewn out of rock. One building looking south to the hills closed off the fourth side. The only but important difference was that here the officers lived in this outside building and could look out their windows over the lower compound to the mountains. It was safe to quarter them there as there was a sixty-foot drop into the lower compound. The back wall held a complex of washrooms, cells for solitary 'confinement, and guardrooms.

We settled down to life in this fortress.

Gavi should have been a depressing place to live in, but it was not. This was because the calibre of the officers, all of whom had escaped once or more, was so high, and their morale so good that the mood was always optimistic, cheerful and courageous. There was no hint of selfishness or bad temper which confinement could bring, and which had often been apparent in the other three prisons where I had been a guest. It was, in fact, like being in a good regiment. Discipline, under the Senior British Officer (SBO), Colonel Fraser, was exemplary. This was also the case among the other ranks who served as batmen. They had all escaped at one time or another, and being individualistic might have been unruly. But Tag Pritchard, a Welch Fusilier parachutist – he indeed who had descended with his parachutists near Padula – was in charge of them and ran them on a loose but effective rein.

It was soon apparent that there was no possibility of escape. We were virtually in a stone box. There was no comparison in security between Gavi and Colditz, where I was to lodge later. Colditz was a building with complicated architecture susceptible to ingenious escape plans. Gavi had no architecture whatever.

And so having 'abandoned all hope' Alastair and I settled down to living the life of a normal prisoner. (Was there such a thing?) I managed to get hold of a German grammar, and every morning after roll call I got down to my studies for three hours. I had found when learning Italian in Nigeria that one hundred hours spent on basics had given me the essential grasp of the language on which to build a vocabulary. And so, within two months I had these basics in German, and progressed to the German discussion group run by Slobodan Drasković, a Jugoslav who had spent much of his life in Germany and had been at Munich University. Ten of us used to meet twice a week, and discuss the war and a variety of other subjects in German. This accustomed our ears to the new sounds and helped us to become idiomatic. Alastair already spoke quite good German and we always conversed in this language when we were together. I learnt German to pass the time. Little did I know how useful it was to be one day.

We had arrived in July. The summer passed. There were no chairs for us at Gavi, so each one of us had bought a cheap and quite comfortable wicker chair from a travelling vendor. These we carried with us wherever we went; and during that beautiful summer we sat on the ramp, looking across the grain-covered plains to the Ligurian mountains and dreamed about what we would do when the war was over.

News was good. First we won the battle of Alamein which began on 23rd October. Then in November came the Allied landing in North Africa. These events were lavishly celebrated with wine which we were allowed to buy twice a week. Morale soared. We thought of nothing but the possibility of the Allies landing in Italy, and of the defeat of Italy. Every day we collected in the courtyard to hear the Italian news howled over a loudspeaker, and it was all good.

Then, one day in January 1943, something happened to take my mind off the battles in Tunis.

One of our batmen was a trooper from my own regiment. Hedley by name. He was employed as a cook, and lived in a room in the lower courtyard directly across from me in the building looking out over the village.

He came up to me one day and asked if he could speak to me in private. I told him to come up to the ramp where he would find me doing my daily fifty turns up and down. He joined me and we walked together.

'I think I may have found a way to break out of here,' he said. I looked at him in blank surprise.

'A way out of here?'

'Well, only maybe,' he replied. 'I'll show you what I've found and then you can see what you think of it.'

In his room the men slept in three-tiered bunks, four bunks – two on each side of the small room. Hedley had one of the top beds, about eight foot from the floor. One night he had turned over and hit his head against the wall. It made a hollow sound, not the flat, hard sound that would be made against the usual stone wall. He told his friend, Leading Seaman McCrae, who had the bunk immediately under him, and they decided to see if they could break through the wall. This they did and they found a hollow shaft on the other side going down 'somewhere'. Rubble was dumped down the shaft.

I should explain here that the Italians did not concern themselves unduly with the security of the batmen. Carabinieri walked through the officers' rooms three or four times a day, sometimes looking in cupboards, or under mattresses, sometimes simply standing in the room for half an hour.

But they almost never went into the batmen's quarters. This meant that Hedley and McCrae had been able to work unobserved, and, as Hedley's bunk was well above eye level, the hole in the wall could not be seen without climbing up to its level. This was lucky as it was about three feet by three feet.

Hedley showed me the hole in the wall and I looked inside. The shaft was also about three feet square. I could see nothing as it was pitch dark. I dropped a stone, hoping to get some idea of its depth. Almost immediately I heard a splash. This meant that the shaft did not go far, and that there was water at the bottom. It was clear that this was a discovery of great importance.

We covered the hole with his greatcoat, and I went back to my quarters to find Alastair.

Obviously we would have to climb down the shaft with a light to see where it went, and whether the water was flowing through a gutter or was in an underground reservoir. We prayed it was the latter.

Next day while Alastair and Hedley held a sheet, I inched my way down the shaft, bracing my bare feet against the side, holding with one hand to the sheet. I had a light made from a pyjama flannel wick soaked in boiled olive oil in my other hand, and this gave a feeble light. The flame did not flicker. Whatever was below had no opening to the outside, that could produce a current of air.

Fifteen feet down, the shaft ended. I was poised there, and I lowered my lamp down as far as I could below the end of the shaft so that I could see.

Four feet below was an expanse of water, but I could not see its limits. But this was enough. I pulled myself back to the top and out through the hole in the wall.

I told Hedley to keep the hole covered by his coat, not to use the shaft, and to get the other men in the room not to talk. Not one of them ever said a word.

It was now pretty clear that Alastair and I could not handle the work that would have to be done alone, so we thought hard who we should bring in.

'We'd better go to the SBO and see what he says about it,' I said to Alastair. Fraser, the SBO, was a young New Zealand colonel, much liked and respected.

'But we don't want him to appoint anyone,' Alastair objected. 'This is a situation where it would be unwise to leave anyone except ourselves to recruit partners.'

He was right, but in the end we decided that we should consult the SBO anyway and hope he would turn over all responsibility to us.

'What a splendid discovery!' was his immediate reaction. 'But you had better get some officers with mining experience to help you. If it goes well, you will need partners used to working underground. Anyway, I leave it to you, but keep me informed as it goes, and I'll do anything I can to help you.'

On this basis four South African officers were automatic choices. Two were mining engineers, Alan Pole and Charles Wuth; and the other two, Buck Palm and Pat Patterson, belonged to the romantic calling of prospectors. Both had dug holes looking for gold, and had worked down them on claims all over South and South-West Africa. All four were just as happy underground as on the surface, and this was something that was definitely not true of Alastair and myself.

When we told them about the project they jumped at it.

'Man,' said Alan Pole, 'we've got an oil compass and a measuring tape' (where had they got them?), 'and we'll go down and make an accurate drawing of what we find.'

Gavi Fortress, Liguria – Part One

We had three roll calls a day and sometimes an extra snap roll call. It was clear that we would have to have a safe warning system when anyone was underground. Our arrangement was to have one of us sit on Hedley's bed with a tin can full of stones as a rattle, and it would be his business to alert anyone down the hole if the bugle sounded for roll call. Roll call was five minutes after the bugle.

Next day Alan Pole and Buck Palm entered the shaft – virtually a chimney – and climbed down. Alastair and I were seated on the bed and we heard two splashes as they dived into the water. Now we had to wait until they came up. In order to make it possible to climb out of the water and up into the shaft, we had managed to secure a rope made of a sheet at the bottom of the shaft and from there it hung down to water level. After about an hour, we heard more splashing as the two swam back to climb up the rope. Then, one after another, they crawled out through the hole in the wall.

They told us what they had found.

One side of the reservoir was formed by the outside wall of the fortress under the batmen's quarters, that is, the wall facing south to the village of Gavi. Pole estimated that this wall, made from huge granite slabs, would be about ten feet thick, and that it lay directly against the roof of the guards' barracks, on the lowest tier of our wedding-cake fortress – we were in the tier above. Water in the reservoir, they said, was about eight feet deep. It was necessary to swim about ten yards to get to the front wall. Also, by the greatest of good fortune, there was a two foot ledge running around the whole reservoir just above water level, thus permitting a man to get out of the water and on to a firm base.

We decided that we would take it in turns to descend the shaft, enter the water, swim to the wall, climb onto the ledge and work for half an hour with an iron bed leg to chip the rock and cut a tunnel two feet square through the wall. Alastair and I were glad we did not have to be responsible for working out how this was to be done. The unique advantage was that any noise of hammering at the rock face could not be heard, isolated as we were in this underground vault many feet above the lowest tier and many feet below the level of the courtyard where we lived.

In early January 1943 we started to work. One of us stood at the gate and watched the movements of any patrolling Carabinieri who entered the compound. Another waited on Hedley's bed ready with his rattle to give warning if the bugle sounded for roll call. And the third man went down into the reservoir to work on the rock face. This system worked well, and, although we had a few narrow squeaks when there was a snap roll call, work went on uninterrupted. But cutting through granite with a sharpened bed leg was immensely hard work and it soon became clear that only the South Africans made real progress. In other words, the work that the rest of us did was only marginally useful and wasted the shift. And so Cram, myself and the two batmen did guard duty on the surface and the South Africans did the heavy work. They never objected because this way we made much quicker progress, which suited everyone. One method we employed was to make a fire on the ledge with wood from the Red Cross parcel crates, heat the rock and then crack it by dousing the rock face with cold water. By doing this we proceeded twice as fast.

One day in February, two guards appeared at the entrance to the compound and brought in a tall, lanky figure whom they escorted to an empty single cell. It was Colonel David Stirling. Almost everyone in the camp had been in North Africa and knew of the raids on Italian and German lines of communication that Stirling had been carrying out with great success for the last fifteen months with his own regiment, the Special Air Service. How did he come to be here?

I had known him slightly before the war and we had many mutual friends. I went along to his cell as soon as the guards left him. It was about ten feet square with no window, just a door leading into the compound.

'How in God's name did you get here?' I asked him. Raiding with small parties behind enemy lines could, and often did, lead to capture, but this was a big fish indeed for the Germans to have caught.

The look of distaste on Stirling's face gave good evidence of his reluctance even to think about it.

'We were operating behind the Mareth line harassing the Germans on their retreat into Tunis and they caught me.' A look of suppressed anger crossed his face.

Apparently he had been lying up in a wadi not far from Gafsa. He had gone there to coordinate SAS operations that were intended not only to harass the retreating German forces, but also to make first contact with the American First Army who were advancing from Algeria. German troops patrolling the area had caught him as he rested with one of his men, but he had managed to bolt from them and to get away. Nevertheless, after walking fifteen miles towards an area where he knew one of his detachments was scheduled to rendezvous, he was betrayed by an Arab. The Arab, speaking a little English, undertook to guide him to the SAS rendezvous he was looking for. In fact, the Arab guided him over a small rise and straight into the hands of a company of Italian infantry. I think that capture by Italians angered Stirling as much as anything else, as he had operated almost entirely against Germans since the start of his SAS career.

When the camp-wide excitement over this new arrival subsided, I asked David to come along to the cell Alastair and I lived in to have a cup of coffee with us.

A very young lieutenant-colonel at the age of twenty-seven, David was about 6 ft 5 in tall, dark, thin and, at the time, wore a moustache. He was dressed in the usual desert uniform, corduroy trousers, suede boots and battledress top. His cap carried the SAS badge of a winged dagger. From his height, he could look down on most people. His eyes were penetrating but friendly. In the next year or so, I observed his eyes turning angry at times, and when they did, the look of anger was very like that of a raven as portrayed in bird books. Extremely affable and with a ready sense of humour, backed by a considerable presence, it was not hard to imagine him as the successful leader that he actually had been during the months of the SAS operations.

Most of us had heard of the SAS raids but that was all we knew. David expanded whilst talking to Alastair and me. Methods of the SAS are now well known and it is hard to realize how imaginative they appeared in those days when the concept was absolutely revolutionary. The story was even more extraordinary when we learnt from David that two years back, as a mere subaltern in the Scots Guards, he had had to convince both General Auchinleck and General Ritchie, orthodox soldiers commanding in the Middle East, that his ideas had merit and to give him authority originally to raise a tiny force of six officers and sixty men. Churchill, of an adventurous spirit similar to David's, had approved and encouraged this initiative, recognizing it as being a means of doing damage to the enemy, while employing only a handful of men.

The concept, forty years later, is still a central one in Britain's overall operational strategy. It is based on the element of surprise.

Small groups of highly trained men were to operate behind enemy lines, destroying planes on the ground, attacking weakly held tactical positions, military and civilian installations, and undertaking raids on enemy headquarters during periods of flux in mobile warfare. Such operations required the highest degree of training and personal initiative among all ranks, and Stirling had been quite ruthless in achieving this level of excellence in his regiment.

It is a matter of interest that fifteen years later I was lunching in Madrid with Colonel Otto Skorzeny, the SS commander responsible, among other remarkable feats, for rescuing Mussolini from Allied hands after the Italian capitulation. He told me that the SAS tactics had been copied lock, stock and barrel by the Germans in a unit set up under his command, a unit that had had wide-ranging success throughout Europe until the end of the war. He was a great fan of Stirling's.

But now, the three of us were sitting in our cold stone cell drinking coffee. I had time to recall what I knew of David's background from before the war. Coming from an old Scottish family, he was, and to a certain extent is today, an unusual mixture of the sophisticate and the exuberant undergraduate, unimpressed by undue solemnity. He had, in fact, been sent down from Cambridge for exhibiting too much of this exuberance.

When I got to know him better, I recognized a very active mind, coupled with an ability to grasp the essential core of a new subject very quickly and to be able to talk about it. Just before the war he had set his sights on climbing Mt Everest. When we started to talk, Alastair found that David, like himself, was a mountaineer. A long discussion then took place in which I could take no part.

Then David broke off and turned to me.

'Is there anyway out of here?' he asked bluntly.

It was a naive question. If there was, no one was going to talk about it. But he was a newcomer and could be forgiven.

'Not as far as we know,' I replied. If we told every friend of ours what we were doing there would be a dozen hangers-on.

'The point is,' he continued headlong,' I simply have to get back to the SAS. My brother Bill is commanding the Second SAS Regiment operating with the American First Army and I want to link up and form an SAS Brigade ready for the coming operations in Europe. I simply have to get out,' he repeated.

David clearly had a better reason than most for getting out, but in a prison like Gavi, he was not unique in wanting to do so. Alastair and I exchanged glances.

'Things happen from day to day,' I said. 'There may be something going on. Why don't you go and talk to the SBO? He has the best overall picture.'

This was an essential first step. We knew that the number assessed as being suitable for the escape was ten. There were the four South Africans, Alastair and myself, and the two batmen, plus Peter Medd and Jerry Daly, who had been prisoners almost since the out break of war, and whom the SBO had selected to make up the ten. It was not up to Alastair or me to invite anyone else into the escape group.

David went back to his cell, and I went to see Colonel Fraser to tell him what had occurred so that he would be prepared. I told him that as far as we were concerned David had all the qualities for joining the party. I left it like that.

The decision would clearly not be an easy one for the SBO. We could imagine that the South Africans who were doing most of

67

the hard work might want to bring in other South Africans. Long-term prisoners with a good record of past escapes might feel that they had a claim. Batmen, who were helping in the cover-up at the entrance to the shaft, might think that they had some right.

It was a measure of the SBO's tact and authority coupled with David's reputation and personality that no opposition surfaced when the SBO decided that David would be the eleventh man. He came in on the project.

CHAPTER FOUR

Gavi Fortess, Liguria – Part Two

The tedious, hard, physical work of chipping a two-feet-square tunnel through the rock face went on throughout February and March without a hitch. Then, one day in early April, Buck Palm called us together. Buck was a huge hulk of a man, powerfully built (he had been at one time a professional wrestler), and he spoke with a strong Afrikaans accent.

'I got through today,' he said. 'Don't be too bloody pleased,' he hurried on as we all started to smile. 'There is a wide strip of electrified barbed wire running in coils over the roof in front of our exit. We have come out precisely on the ridge pole of the guards' barracks on the level below. But there is no chance of getting through onto the roof unless we can get some insulated wire cutters.'

Gloom settled on us. However, I had an idea. I had made it my business ever since arriving at Gavi to make friends with any of the guards who were not afraid to talk, which most of them were. However, with an invasion of Italy clearly imminent, attitudes were changing rapidly, and I had formed a fairly good relationship with a lugubrious Genovese called Prato. He had started to pass on to me forbidden BBC news, and we discussed openly what might happen to Italy after the defeat that everyone saw coming. I told the escape team that I would try to induce Prato to get us a pair of wire cutters. I approached him the following night. He was on guard in a dark corner of the compound. We exchanged whispered greetings.

'You know,' I said, 'when the Allies get here you guards will be given a bad time as Gavi is known as a punishment camp.'

69

'*É vero, Maggiore,*' he agreed.

'I can get a letter from the SBO that will protect you, but I want something in exchange.'

I did not tell him why I wanted wire cutters, but I said if he could get me a pair, I would give him what money he needed. To my great surprise he agreed immediately.

'But I cannot buy them here. I'll have to wait until I get a few days' leave and go home to Genoa. I do not know when that will be.'

There was nothing to be done but to wait, but luckily not for long. He didn't come on guard for nearly a week, but when he arrived back he had them. I paid him and gave him an extravagantly grateful letter from the SBO that I put into Italian, as well as a present of 10,000 lire. Perhaps we would need him again, I thought.

*

Now we were ready to go. We had all saved chocolate, raisins and biscuits from our Red Cross parcels for months to put in our haversacks. We had maps, homemade compasses, and each of us had put together some sort of mongrel kit to look like a civilian. In my case, I had an olive-green Greek soldier's jacket, and a blue air force shirt, black tie and black armband to indicate mourning. My trousers were the corduroys I had been captured in. My heavy boots were Italian, very good quality, made in Venice and bought in the camp from a merchant who visited us once a month.

The important thing now was to plan what we would do when we were on the roof and through the wire. This was made easy for us because, from the window of the batmen's quarters, we looked down directly onto the area we would have to navigate. We could see our obstacles quite plainly.

First was the roof. This was tiled, steep and covered by two machine guns, one in each of two battlement turrets about thirty yards either side. The ridge-pole had to be traversed, and then it would be necessary to slide down the tiles on one side of the roof where a high wall was accessible with a small jump. This wall ran around the lower compound where wooden huts housed the guards. We would have to walk along the top of this wall and climb down from it into the compound itself where it ended against a disused turret on the battlements. Once inside the compound, we would have to cross to where a sapling grew in front of the battlements. The leading escaper would have the task of fixing a rope to the sapling so that we could lower ourselves by the rope thirty feet down to the rocky, steep hillside below.

Because the roof onto which we would emerge from our tunnel was covered by machine guns, we needed a rainy night for the escape. On a really bad night, we had observed that the guards pulled down their caps, huddled in their coats and relaxed their vigilance. So weather had to dictate the night for our move.

We waited. Every night was a clear night. Would it never rain?

Eventually we had luck. At five one evening in April a dense mist settled on the fortress, and not only that, it started to rain heavily.

We decided that the break should take place at 10 pm, halfway through the guards' four-hour tour of duty, when they would neither be fresh from having just arrived nor alert waiting for their relief. Michael Pope, a naval officer in my room, had unselfishly agreed to come with us as far as the exit to replace the stone slab when we left so that there would be no indication as to how we got out. If we succeeded, the exit would be used again and Pope would be the leader.

At about 9.30 pm the escape party assembled in Hedley's room. This was no problem as we could come and go freely in the courtyard and guards were used to this. We hung our clothes around our necks, climbed down the shaft, swam to the ledge and got into our clothes again. The four South Africans led. Palm first, after them Cram, Stirling, myself, Daly, Medd, and finally the two batsmen, Hedley and McRae. My task, placed in the middle, was to act as liaison between possible trouble for the leaders in front and possible trouble for the followers in the rear.

Palm was to remove the stone shielding the tunnel, cut the wire and make a clear passage. He crawled into the tunnel and we all stood fully clothed again on the ledge in correct order, waiting.

We were shivering with anticipation and excitement as much as from our ice-cold swim.

Within fifteen minutes Palm had cleared a gap through the wire and was out. We crawled through after him one by one. When I got onto the roof, David, in front of me, was already half-way along the ridge. It was reassuring to see that the machine guns on either side were hardly visible in spite of the floodlighting. I crawled along the roof top, slid down over the tiles and jumped onto the battlement wall. The wall, high where I jumped, ran down gradually to a height of three feet.

As I reached the compound level I could see Stirling ahead of me striding rapidly towards the sapling and the rope. Suddenly a door in one of the huts opened, and half a dozen soldiers, singing and apparently drunk, came out. Heads down against the rain, they walked passed David without pausing, and entered another hut. They were followed by a dozen more. These spotted David's tall figure as he ran towards the battlement, and in a moment had surrounded him, shouting. Sirens started up and a few rifle shots went off somewhere.

I glanced behind me and saw Medd, Daly and the two batmen stranded along the rooftop.

David broke through the guard and ran along the battlement with a crowd of soldiers now pouring out of their huts in pursuit. As he ran, he struck out at them.

It was clear now that I had to look after myself.

No one had noticed me yet. I walked slowly over to the rope in order not to attract attention, grasped it and dropped over the battlements, falling thirty feet: the rope had broken. My fall was fortunately cushioned by the steep incline of the rocky hill. I wasn't hurt but I lost my knapsack with documents, maps, compass and food.

Picking myself up, I half slid and half ran down the hill towards Gavi village at the bottom. I could hear a few rifle shots, searchlights were roaming the walls and sirens were wailing. The scene was chaotic but I didn't spend much time observing it.

My object was to get through the village, wade the river that ran along the far side, and then take stock of my situation. I had no time to think about what had happened to the others. In spite of the commotion high up at the fortress, the village slept peacefully. There was no one in the streets, and I arrived at the river unchallenged, waded through it, and sat down in a clump of bushes to consider what I should do.

Although I had lost food, maps and compass in my fall, I still had a good supply of money. Clearly there was no point in sticking to our original plan of walking to the Swiss border and crossing at Zermatt. Alastair and David were to lead on this march and I had neither the knowledge nor supplies to attempt it on my own. One thing was certain: there would be a massive search. I could reasonably be expected to go north towards Switzerland, so my first decision was to go south over the Ligurian hills towards Genoa and the coast. I felt sure the searchers would not look in that direction. What would be the point in going south?

My second decision was to stay close to Gavi for twenty-four hours. I was sure the search party would be working outward and further afield. An escaped prisoner would not be expected to stay put outside his prison, and, for the moment, my first concern was to keep free until the excitement died down.

And so I found a small wood with very thick undergrowth near by on the river, and there I hid, half a mile from the fortress, all the next day until dark. It continued to rain, and I was wet and cold, but I was happy. Girls tending geese came near to my hide-out several times. When they did, I entered the river and stayed submerged except for my head, concealed by overhanging bushes, until they went away. No soldiers searched the area.

When darkness came I started on my journey south across the mountains to the Mediterranean coast. The rain had stopped.

People in these remote mountain valleys lived very isolated lives. They raised the food they needed for themselves, and one visit a month with a donkey would bring them the salt, flour and other staples they needed from the nearest village, otherwise they seldom left their valleys. An occasional forest ranger might be encountered, but with luck I would not be challenged, as long as

I could explain the accent in my Italian. This I decided to do by explaining that I was a German deserter from a working party. It was a ruse that I had used on my previous wanderings in Southern Italy; it had worked then, and I hoped it would work again. By now I knew that most Italian peasants were sympathetic to anyone who was trying to avoid the Axis war effort.

For the next two days I walked along mountain tracks, taking any track that went in a southerly direction. I had only one objective, which was to reach the coast near Genoa where I could make a plan based on using the money I had. Sometimes I would come to a house in a fertile patch of valley where I could see the peasant landowner tending his sheep or ploughing. I avoided these; but on the second day I decided I would have to get something to eat – water had been plentiful in mountain streams but I had had no food.

At about three in the afternoon I arrived at an open plateau where I could see a small hamlet of a dozen poor houses, and a green where some ten men were playing the Italian equivalent of boule. The place was so remote that I decided to be bold, and approach them. In case of trouble I could run.

I walked slowly across the pasture to the green where they were playing. Soon I was spotted, and they stopped their game to stare. It was an awkward moment.

I walked up to the group. The game was being played outside a small wine shop. There was a wood and a steep valley behind it – a good place to run if things went wrong.

'Good evening,' I said. 'Who is winning?'

The winner pointed to himself. No one said anything but they all stood watching, old men, youths, and a few crones. Such people were so parochial that I risked shocking them into interest with a huge lie.

'It is tiring walking over these mountains,' I said. 'I am a German deserter, and I don't want to go back to Germany. My mother is Italian. She has relatives who live near Genoa. That is where I am going.'

The flood gates of curiosity then opened. Where had I escaped?

How long ago? Why had my mother married a German? Had I had anything to eat? I admitted I hadn't, and offered to buy some wine and cheese from the little shop. Bread was rationed and out of the question without a ration card.

'*Poverino!*' Poor man, exclaimed one of the crones and disappeared into the shop. There was no hostility or suspicion amongst the bystanders so I started to chat with them. Would I join the game?

While we played I learnt that the path I was taking would lead to a valley where the Turin–Genoa train ran – about five miles away. There was a small station where workers from a nearby village boarded the train every day early to go to work in Genoa. This was vital information as it meant that I could join the train amongst a crowd of other travellers.

When our game was over the crone appeared from the shop with some bread, goat's cheese and a flask of wine for me. We sat around talking and, as usual, discussed the war. I told them all about Germany (where I had never been). I liked these people and I liked them even more after I had finished the litre of wine.

At about five o'clock, with morale raised by the food and wine, I said goodbye and set off along a path that the Italians indicated. There would be three more hours of daylight, and I wanted to be on the hill looking down onto the valley where the train ran before nightfall.

Just before dark I mounted a rise and below me was the valley with the railway clearly visible winding through it. I could see a small village – it must be there that workers boarded the train. But I had to know the time the trains ran. I could not risk hanging around in a village where a stranger would attract attention amongst the workers, who probably knew each other. So I looked for a farm and found one. A young woman opened the door at my knock. Was her husband in? I asked, hoping he was not. No, he was in the army. Well, could she help, I went on. I had been promised work in Genoa, and was on my way there. Could she tell me if the Turin train stopped at the small village in the valley? What time was the earliest train in the morning? Half past five, she told me. That was all I needed to know. I thanked her and left.

This was the train I must take, and I retired into nearby woods to spend the night. But out of excitement and fear of not waking at the right time, I could not sleep, and spent the night walking about. I reckoned that it would take me half an hour to get down to the station. So just before five I set out, timing my pace so as to arrive at the station with only enough time to buy my ticket. I wanted to avoid having to chat with the workers.

My timing was good. I arrived five minutes before the train, bought my ticket and boarded an open cattle truck with about thirty workers. I engaged a girl in conversation so as not to appear a stranger. Strangely enough I excited no curiosity, and half an hour later I got out at the central station of Genoa. I had achieved my first objective. I was free in a big, anonymous city with money in my pocket. It was the Thursday before Easter 1943.

Genoa railway station was fully of early morning traffic. No one had time or inclination to look around. There were the usual Carabinieri, observant and strolling in pairs, but I was pretty sure that I would not be looked for, fifty miles south of Gavi. For the moment I felt safe.

I found a bench quite near the station and sat down to take stock.

I was not happy with my Greek soldier's jacket: I would have to steal a civilian one or a sweater. As far as money was concerned I had enough for any rail fare I might need, as well as enough to buy what food was available in small working-class restaurants. I knew that spaghetti, rice, bread and meat were all rationed but that minestrone, fish and ersatz chocolate were not. Neither was beer and wine. So I would be all right as far as food and drink were concerned. I had lost maps and compass, but I had a good idea of the geography of Northern Italy and I could decide on a travel plan later. I had no documents and this was serious. I needed some sort of cover.

In order to have a cover story, I decided to pose as a Croat. Croatia along with Slovenia was the only province of Jugoslavia that was pro-Italian; no one knew much about it, and my foreign accent in Italian or in German would be explained away if I came from a country whose language no one could speak anyway.

This decided, I went back to the station and from the news-stand bought a *Voelkischer Beobachter*, official organ of the Nazi Party, and a *Giornale d'Italia*, ditto of the Italian Fascist Party. With these prominently displayed under my arm I hoped to be identified by passers-by as a good supporter of the Axis. It worked very well.

I anticipated that I would be around for some days, and if this was so, replacing my Greek jacket had to be a priority. I would have to find something better.

Before the war I had been in Genoa, and when I got out at the station I knew where I was. I was close to the dockside and even closer to the brothel area, this side of it – handy for seamen. I set out for this district.

Eight o'clock in the morning is not a busy time for brothels, and the narrow alleys were nearly deserted. What I was looking for, and what I found, was the laundry of the locals strung up as is usual in all Latin countries from houses on one side of the street on lines fixed to houses on the other side.

In a quarter of an hour I saw what I needed: an old sweater hanging on a line. No one was about. I climbed a lamp post, pulled down the clothes line and took the sweater, transferring my black armband to it. Then I quickly made off.

It had now been nearly four days since I left Gavi. I had not had much sleep and what I had was snatched lying soaking wet in the woods – fitful sleep and full of half-waking fears. It seemed to me that a few hours' rest would be a good investment. So I made my way to Genoa Cathedral near to the station. I found a dark corner close to the organ and knelt down, resting my head in my hands. I went to sleep at once, but my nerves and the clock inside my head woke me in about two hours. Now I would have to think of my move to the Swiss frontier.

From a close study of maps while at Gavi, and fortunately also from some travel in Northern Italy before the war, I had a fair knowledge of its geography. I knew that just north of Milan there were two lakes, each forming a frontier with Switzerland. One was Como, the natural objective of an escaper (and of Italian black marketeers) with a narrow frontier running along flat land – heavily guarded. This was too obvious to risk. The other alternative was Lake Maggiore.

Lake Maggiore was half in Italy and half in Switzerland. At the top end was the Swiss town of Locarno. At the bottom, that is the southern end, was the small Italian town of Verbania Pallanza. I had travelled by rail from Venice through Milan to Paris before the war. I remembered that on this trip before entering the Domodossola tunnel the train had stopped at Verbania Pallanza for a few minutes. That meant that if I could get there, I could be only twenty miles from the Swiss border on the west side of the lake. I came to the conclusion that I should go from Genoa to Milan and then to Verbania Pallanza – the whole trip by rail, and fast.

Meanwhile I was free; I had money; and I decided to look around Genoa, see what bombing damage we had done, in case I got back to England, and talk to some of the locals in order to tune in on their views about the war. I had talked to guards before but not to a civilian. This was a chance to do it.

Around noon I went into a small shabby restaurant near the water front. I ordered minestrone and a grappa, and opened my German newspaper.

Two German soldiers came in and sat at the next table. They tried to order a meal but spoke no Italian, so I helped them. With their coupons they could buy bread, cheese and spaghetti. Each of them ordered three bottles of beer.

'You're not German,' one of them said to me, looking at the German paper I had been reading.

'No,' I replied. 'I'm from Croatia but I like to read the German papers because I worked in Germany and like the people.'

'Don't you like the Italians?'

'They're all right but they aren't soldiers. I don't think you have very useful allies.'

Both soldiers smiled.

'They are more trouble than they are worth. Hitler is a great man but he made a big mistake when he teamed up with Mussolini.'

I agreed. They offered me a beer and we talked about the war. They were on their way back to Germany from Tunis. The British were good soldiers, they thought. Americans were undisciplined, but they had marvellous equipment. They also were paid a great deal, so they had heard. Soon they said goodbye and left. I ordered a coffee and went back to my paper.

The little Italian waiter came over to me.

'You speak good Italian for a German.'

'I'm not a German. I'm a Croat.'

'Oh, I see. Germans are rough people. I don't know why we went into the war with them. Personally I like the English. I worked in a restaurant in San Remo before the war. They gave very big tips, the English. Germans never gave anything.'

I asked for the bill. As I paid I thought what a good commentary I had been given on the Axis friendship.

I spent the afternoon walking around the city. It had been my intention to see the damage our bombers had done to the harbour, but I had to give this up because I could see that the nearer I got to the dockside the more police there were. I could do no good hanging around, and decided to leave for Milan the next day.

At six o'clock in the evening when the station was busiest I went to the ticket office and bought a return ticket to Milan. I bought a return ticket because two Carabinieri were watching the ticket queue and a return ticket would not be suspect. Then I looked at the time table and decided to take a slow train that would leave at 11 am next day, stopping all along the line. This seemed safest in case for some reason I had to get off and run for it before reaching Milan.

I had a leisurely dinner in another small and modest restaurant, this time grilled sardines and squid with a bottle of red wine. Afterwards I went to a cinema to pass the time, and when

I got out I returned to my church and slept until dawn in the darkest corner.

From then until train time I kept on the move, walking in the busiest part of the town after having a breakfast of more sardines, coffee and a grappa. At the same time I bought three bars of chocolate as a reserve ration.

As it was Easter the train which I boarded was packed, standing room only, and I waited until the last possible moment to avoid being engaged in conversation. Standing in the corridor I could hardly move, and stood looking out of the open window with my back to the crowd. This suited me very well. The trip was going to take about two hours, stopping every fifteen or twenty minutes, and my main worry was the possibility of a check on documents. But I knew that checks on these slow commuter trains were not routine as they were on the faster trains. I hoped to be lucky.

One of the stations was Aquata Scrivia. There I had the pleasure of seeing Gavi fortress outlined against the horizon about three miles away. I was not tempted to get off.

I was standing at the very front end of my carriage. After about one hour I heard the dreaded words *'Documenti, signori'* called out by two ordinary police who had entered at the rear of the train.

My guess was that it would take ten, perhaps fifteen minutes to go through the entire carriage full of travellers. It was likely that these were the only police on this small commuter train. So I moved down the crowded corridor from my window position to the next carriage forward. Now I could only wait and hope that we would stop at the next station before the police arrived. In about ten minutes the train started to slow down, and at the same time I could hear the voices of the police in the car to my rear approaching. It was a bad moment.

At last the train pulled into a fair-sized station, Voghera. I shouldered my way through the crowd to the door and dismounted with quite a few others. Then I walked slowly back to the last carriage of the train. Just as it left I got on board again. The police were now moving away from me through the carriages; but would they come back? and how long before we would get to Milan? I dared not ask.

The next hour was too full of suspense for my liking. However an elderly woman next to me asked if I would help her get her parcels off at the next stop – she had so many. What was the next stop? I asked. Milan she told me. I said, yes, I would help, and indeed partnering an old woman in Milan station suited me very well. We got off the train together, both laden with parcels.

Milan station was a very different proposition to Genoa, being a major terminal connecting trains from the north, south, east and west. Moreover, it was the nearest major city to Switzerland. There were Carabinieri and Blackshirt police everywhere, each ticket queue under surveillance. My best hope it seemed to me was to keep my friend talking as long as possible while I looked at the departure board for the next train to Stresa, Verbania Pallanza and Domodosolla. By the greatest of good fortune one was leaving in twenty minutes. The lady with the parcels said goodbye and left. Now I had to buy my ticket alone.

Standing in a queue to get to the ticket counter was not a good experience. Carabinieri stood by the counter and could hear the station for which a ticket was bought. As I got close to the ticket counter my heart was pounding. At the last moment I decided to buy a return ticket to Stresa which was less close to the Swiss border than Verbania Pallanza. At Stresa I would buy another return ticket, this time a local one to Pallanza. Carabinieri would be less interested in a traveller to Stresa.

All went well. I got my ticket, and walked slowly away looking dejected and preoccupied. I believe my black armband had been a real help in discouraging any talk or questions. Looking depressed had proved to be a good disguise. The train was waiting, almost empty. I got into a compartment alone, and took out my German newspaper. It was a beautiful sunny April afternoon and I felt pleased as the train pulled out and headed for Stresa. But I was apprehensive about document examination. There would be no question of using the same ruse on this train as it was empty and Stresa was the second stop.

The first hour out of Milan we passed along flat countryside, pleasantly green with the new crops and fruit tree blossoms. Then came our first stop and I looked out into the empty corridor to see if any police got onto the train. None did. There were few new passengers. One got into my carriage and settled down at the window seat in the apartment I was occupying. She was a pretty girl carrying a cardboard hatbox, and I sat down next to her, wishing as always to be thought of as someone travelling with a friend.

We talked and looked out the window as the train started to run along the edge of Lake Maggiore towards Stresa. She was a Milan milliner's assistant bringing a hat to a client in Stresa. She had a French glossy magazine full of fashion pictures which she showed me. When she heard I had been to Paris she asked all about it. Was it true that the whole city was underground? I explained that you travelled underground on the Metro, but you lived above ground. This relieved her mind. She couldn't understand it, she said.

Suddenly I heard '*Documenti, signori*' called at the back of the carriage. As there were few travellers, I knew that the man would soon arrive at our compartment. Whatever I did I would have to do quickly.

I trusted to the romantic temperament of the Italian male. I put my right arm across the seat behind the girl's shoulders, turned my back to the sliding door that formed the compartment entrance, put my face close to the girl, who thought I was intent on looking at pictures in the magazine in her lap, and waited. To anyone entering the compartment I hoped that from his angle we would look like fond lovers. (It was many years later that I was told that this was exactly what Robert Donat had done when in similar trouble in the film *The Thirty-nine Steps*.)

I heard footsteps outside in the corridor. They stopped and my heart nearly did too. I moved my head even closer to the girl's. The door slid open.

For a moment there was a pause. Then I heard the door sliding shut. There was a cough, and then '*Buon giorno*' – good day, said this splendid, sensitive man as he moved on up the carriage.

But from then on I was extremely nervous and much relieved when we arrived at Stresa.

I got off, carrying the girl's hatbox. It was my intention to get her to look up the time of the next train for my destination at Pallanza, and also to buy a ticket for me so that I would avoid standing in line. There was bound to be Carabinieri about.

I suggested that we have a coffee. She agreed and we went into the bar. There I said that I had to telephone Genoa, which might take some time. While I was doing this, would she buy my ticket and check the next departure? I gave her the money and left the bar. After walking around the block a few times, I returned. She had my ticket: the next train left in about an hour.

We had another coffee, toasted each other (our romance?) in a cognac, exchanged addresses – hers in Milan, mine in Gavi (a nice touch I thought), and said goodbye.

For an hour I walked along the lakeside to pass the time. It was about six in the evening and the sun was just setting behind Mont Blanc to the west, a perfectly beautiful sunset. I felt exhilarated, and fairly confident that I might now make the frontier. Still, there was the short trip to Pallanza, and the ever-present danger of a document check so near the border.

I need not have worried. I went into a lavatory as soon as the train left, opened the window as a possible exit in case of trouble, and only came out when we arrived at Pallanza. No one else got off.

It was getting dark, but it was still light enough for me to see where the lake was, and I knew that the road to the frontier and to Locarno ran north along the western shore. I set off to walk the twenty-five miles, reckoning it better to go fast along the road than to try and climb across the mountains that formed the frontier running west–east to the lake. First I ate my three bars of chocolate.

Fortune was with me. The road had virtually no traffic on it, and by one o'clock in the morning I had arrived at Intra. I had read about Intra in Hemingway's book *A Farewell to Arms*, and remembered how easily he had crossed the border by boat. I could see the lights of Locarno but I had no boat. It was clear that the lake was policed by launches, as I could see searchlights blinking out on the lake, probably checking on fishing boats.

Much to my surprise I encountered no problems in getting through Intra. The streets were nearly deserted, everything was quiet, and a bright moon gave light for me to read the signs that pointed the way out of the town to the Locarno road.

Along the way I passed the houses of rich Milan, Budapest and Munich millionaires. I wanted to get into one of their gardens to rest, but for the first time I realized how carefully the rich guarded their properties. There were high walls, huge iron gates firmly locked, iron fences with barbed wire on top – hopeless. I walked on until dawn.

With first light I realized I was within five miles of the frontier. Now I would have to decide whether to cross it by going off the road and back into the mountains, or to swim one or two miles around the Italian frontier post at night. It seemed to me that for the moment the right thing to do would be to rest. I had had very little sleep for nearly a week and was beginning to feel light-headed. I would decide my route later.

Soon I saw what I wanted, a long, very thick clump of rhodo-dendrons sloping from the road down to the lakeside. I crawled through them to the water's edge and lay down. Immediately I went to sleep.

I was awoken by someone shaking me. I jumped up into the arms of two Carabinieri. It was late afternoon and I had slept for eight hours. The Carabinieri were making a patrol of the shoreline. What I had done – slept for nearly one whole day – was so awful that I could not bear to think of it. I was numb with disappointment.

My captors took me along to the frontier police station and their chief telephoned Gavi to say they had caught me. Then they gave me a magnificent meal, lots of wine and locked me up in a cell with a good bed. Next day I started my return trip – Stresa, Milan, Gavi – the wrong direction.

But going back in the train I thought about what had happened. There I was lying in a dense thicket of rhododendrons thirty yards from the road, right on the lake edge, well concealed, and yet I had been found by a Carabinieri patrol. I couldn't understand it. I talked to my guards who were from Intra police station.

'Do Carabinieri always patrol through that plantation of rhododendrons?' I asked.

'No,' was the reply.

'Why were they there that day?'

The two guards looked at each other and remained silent.

'Why?' I persisted.

Eventually one of them answered.

'They were looking for a blackmarket smuggler who escaped two days ago from a prison in Milan. The Carbinieri thought that he might try to cross the frontier right where you were. Bad luck,' he had the decency to add. 'It's a good place to do it.'

This only added to the intense disappointment I already felt. But for the smuggler, there was no question I would have made it, and the rest of the war would have been very different for me. As it was, I subsided in a corner of the baggage car and sulked until we got back to Gavi.

I was greeted as the wrong kind of celebrity by officers and guards when I got back. According to them, we had been the first to break out of Gavi for 600 years; and I had been out for ten days. The officer on night duty when we broke out was being court-martialled and the guards in the courtyard had already been given long sentences in the cooler. I asked if any others were still out but got no reply. Of course our exit route had been discovered and sealed off once they realized we had come out over the roof.

The Commandant gave me a long interrogation. Two companies of Alpini troops had apparently been turned out to look for us the day after the escape. (So I had been right not to move!) How could I stay free for over a week unless I had friends? Who were these friends? Without documents I could never have got as far as the frontier. Someone must have provided me with documents. Etcetera, etcetera.

I had been through this kind of thing before and fended off the questions until they gave up. The interview ended with a sentence of thirty days' solitary – not much of a punishment.

As I was marched off to the cell I saw Alastair Cram and David Stirling looking out through the iron grille. I shouted: was anyone still out? No, came the reply; the South Africans and Cram had been rounded up by Alpini north of Gavi. All the others had been caught on the lower level before getting out.

It had been a good week, but it had a really bad end.

*

By the time I was released from solitary it was nearly June. By then the Germans and Italians had been driven out of North Africa, and for us who were in Italy and who had a feeling of the country's mood, it looked pretty certain that Italy would soon capitulate or be forced to surrender. We thought – quite wrongly as it turned out – that the Germans would withdraw north into Austria behind the Alps, leaving Italy to the Allies as a defeated nation. With these ideas in our minds there were no more thoughts of escape. Two or three months would not be long to wait for our freedom, and we listened to the courtyard radio broadcast every day with increasing confidence.

In July Badoglio deposed Mussolini; and in August – as history now relates – started to treat for surrender in secret. We were in a state of high excitement, certain that Italy would soon be out of the war – one way or another.

Behind the scenes negotiations went on which are now well known and on 8th September 1943 Badoglio's Italy capitulated. The senior British Officer met the Camp Commandant and told him we would stay put in an orderly manner until the British arrived to take over. There were German troops in Italy but we could not imagine them wasting time and manpower on prisoners of war, when, as we assumed, they would be occupied in withdrawing north.

We were correct in general, but not in particular. As was later confirmed, the German High Command had already ordered that Gavi alone among all the prison camps in Italy was to be occupied immediately and all inmates transported to Germany. This was because we were supposed to be dangerous and might engage in sabotage. Other camps were simply ignored. At the time we intended to await the arrival of British troops. (British troops in fact only arrived at Gavi eighteen months later.) Even so we were made uneasy by seeing German troops passing to and fro that day through Gavi. But they left us alone, and, we were sure, they had more important things to do than involve themselves with prisoners of war. That evening the whole camp celebrated with wine, songs – 'The Maori Farewell' for the New Zealanders, 'The Zulu Warrior' for South Africans, 'Waltzing Matilda' for the Australians and 'It's a Long Way to Tipperary' for all of us. The Italian guards looked on benignly. I told Prato who had got me the wire clippers that we would see him well rewarded. We went to bed happy, planning our futures when we would be back in England and able to get into action again.

The next morning we awoke at dawn to see a company of German soldiers advancing up the hill from Gavi village. A few Italians fired at them, and were cut down by return machine-gun fire. Smoke mortar bombs were fired at the Commandanture. The Germans had surrounded the fortress during the night and very soon the Italian Commandant hoisted the white flag.

It is impossible to describe how we felt. Instead of being free we were new guarded by men who, even though not trained to guard prisoners, were infinitely more resolute than the Italians they had replaced. And Germany was our destination for sure. Everyone now started to try to find a way out on his own, counting on the Germans not to know the castle's lay-out as we did. Tunnels were started, roofs were reconnoitred. But no one had managed to carry out his plan – although many were very near completion – when, a week later, on Monday 13th September, we were told that we were to move to Germany in an hour.

Chaos followed. Prisoners hid themselves with stocks of food in all manner of places prepared during the previous week – in cellars, between roofs and ceilings, in sewers. One officer lodged himself in a chimney. We believed that the Germans had no list of the number of prisoners in the castle to check on roll call so hiding was worth a try.

The Germans, until then rather indolent and uninterested guards, now tore the place apart. Open season was declared on our Red Cross parcels, clothes, and bedding – everything was looted. Stirling, Cram and myself had dislodged a lavatory seat and had found a cavity twenty feet square underneath filled with pipes.

Here we hid with our food stocks. For two days we listened as noises came to us from the courtyard above, mainly shouting as only Germans can shout. Sometimes we heard faint English voices which meant that the camp had not yet been evacuated; and this was worrying. The Germans were clearly persisting and were not going away without a very thorough search. The longer we waited the more worried we became, as we had anticipated hiding for only a short time, and we had had no time to bring water with us. Time passed slowly but we were kept alert due to the continuous racket above us.

Then, on the second day, we heard hammering and German voices in the lavatory above us. The hammering became insistent and we retreated into the farthest corner behind the maze of pipes. It was no use. Great blows were struck at the floor above the lavatory basin and eventually a grenade was thrown at it. The explosion filled our corner with thick dust. We all started to cough. Almost immediately a torch was shone through the opening blown into the cavity, and a German soldier dropped through it, machine pistol in his hand at the ready.

' *'Raus oder ich schiesse!*' he shouted.

There was no doubt that he would shoot, and so I came forward and replied that we had no weapons and would come out.

It turned out that we were the last to be discovered, and so after a night when the whole camp was herded into the courtyard and slept on the cobbles, a detachment of the German Feldpolizei appeared and marshalled us into trucks.

The Feldpolizei wore nickel plaques hung around their necks on chains and were ruthless customers. They were the troops that herded Jews to Polish extermination camps, were notoriously quick on the trigger and had no 'Geneva Convention ethics'. We knew that no one could expect any quarter from them if he stepped out of line, and we sat sullenly in the trucks as we drove east to Mantua. There we were dumped into an athletics stadium, floodlit and covered all around the oval with machine guns. The next day we were marched to a train and loaded into cattle trucks. We were bound for Austria.

CHAPTER FIVE

Innsbruck, Markt Pongau, Berlin, Eichstätt

Our train had attracted a crowd of local Italians who stood watching us being loaded. They threw oranges, grapes, and loaves of bread for us and shouted good wishes. When we had been loaded, the door of the cattle truck was temporarily left open, and I shouted at some of the Italian men asking them to go along the train and spot where the machine guns were sited that would guard the train. We were safe talking Italian. The men said it was too dangerous, that the Germans would stop them.

Then a handsome blonde woman of about forty pushed her way to the front. The German guarding the door to our truck tried to stop her, threatening her with his rifle. She pushed it aside and came right up to the door. Exactly what did I want to know? she asked. In spite of the shouting and threats of the guard she stood listening as I explained, and then walked off heading towards the front of the train. Soon she came back and pushed her way past the sentry again, coming right up to where I was standing.

'There is a machine gun mounted on the front and back of the roof of every cattle truck, but I don't think their field of fire is good close to the trucks. Good luck to all of you.' She pushed past the sentry and went back into the crowd. '*Che ragazza meravigliosa!*' as the Italians would say.

Soon the doors clanged shut and the train moved off. We started to pry planks loose from the wall and from the floor of our truck and were making progress when, after two or three hours, the train stopped and a guard opened the door. We were to get out and relieve ourselves. Feldpolizei were all around us with threatening automatic rifles.

In the next car to us were some Italians being deported to Germany as forced labour. Two of these men for some reason started to leave their group and to walk in our direction. Without warning a burst from the automatic rifles cut them down. They were not dead, but lay screaming in agony on the ground with their stomachs spilling out. A Feldwebel came running. He took his pistol and shot each Italian in the head. Even then one of them did not die, but lay twitching on the ground.

We looked on, stunned. We were prepared to be shot on the run, but not to be murdered after capture. We decided that we would not try to escape – not now anyway.

However, Alastair was wilier than David or myself. Our next stop was at the small town of Mezza Coronna, just short of the Brenner Pass. Once the door to the truck opened, Alastair, huddled up in a corner started howling.

'I can't stand it!' he screamed. '*Aiuto, aiuto,* help! Please, a doctor, I beg of you!'

Alastair made such a hideous and convincing noise that soon the guard appeared with a Red Cross nurse.

'It's my stomach,' moaned Alastair. 'Here, here, oh please – it must be my appendix.'

In due course two stretcher bearers appeared and Alastair was carted off to hospital. The local hospital of course had no security arrangements, so that very night – as we learnt some months later – he escaped from the hospital and was eventually re-captured en route to join the Jugoslav partisans. Really good quick thinking – well worthy of my old partner.

The train moved off again and around five in the evening stopped at the Brenner Pass. Here the Feldpolizei stood down and guard duty was taken over by soldiers of the Wehrmacht. David and I went on the alert again as the train wound its way down to Innsbruck. We were prepared to take on the Wehrmacht. The Feldpolizei, it had to be admitted, had really scared us.

Arriving in Austria David and I now faced up to the fact that we had failed to escape in Italy at a time when, after the capitulation, there was a real chance of staying free, and that we were now in Hitler's Third Reich which, according to him, would last one thousand years. We were not really concerned with those one thousand years, but we reckoned we could well be looking at another five before it was all over, and that was quite enough.

The train rattled into Innsbruck station and halted. A guard entered the truck and counted us. When he left he did not bolt the sliding door, even leaving it slightly open so that we could see the movement of soldiers on the platform and could hear a lot of talking and shouting. But soon everything became quiet. Peering out, we could see no one on the platform where we had been shunted.

It took no time for David and me to slide open the door and get out. It was raining and misty. Ahead of us, we could dimly see a goods yard with a lot of rolling stock but no soldiers. Behind us we were aware that three others had followed us, but we were not concerned with them. Our concern was what to do next.

The first problem was to try to fix in our minds where Innsbruck actually was. Neither of us had ever been in Austria and didn't know its geography. All we knew was that the Inn river, which flowed through the town, rose in Switzerland which we judged to be about 100 miles to the west of us. Train travel was out of the question as we had no money.

These thoughts were foremost in our minds as we ran through the goods yard. Fortunately the town was blacked out because of Allied air attacks on Brenner rail traffic, so that few people were about. That day our train had run from the Brenner Pass down through the wooded mountains into Innsbruck. Now we headed back through the town in the direction of those same mountains, hoping to hide and gain a momentary respite.

Innsbruck, with its Baroque architecture, is not a very big place. Soon we had crossed the River Inn with its bridge to the south side. We threaded our way through narrow streets and reached woods and pasture land just above the town. There we sat down in the wood to make a plan.

We had only the clothes we stood up in and nothing else, so we would have to walk. This left us with no alternative but to travel west towards Switzerland, traversing the foothills of the Tyrol and using the river below as our point of reference. But walking in this

Alpine country would be slow going, and we had to face the fact that in such country, a march of 100 miles could well take us a week. Without food this was not a good bet. Eventually we decided to traverse the foothills by day and to descend into the river valley by night, following the road we were able to see when next morning it became light. This way we would make better time, and hoped we might be able to get to the Swiss frontier in three days. David, with his experience of mountains, would lead by day. I would deal with any encounter we might have at night when passing through small villages in the valley.

For two days and one night, we made good progress. David plotted a fairly painless course for us along pastures below the tree line, and we passed at night through half a dozen villages on the valley road with no trouble. We tried to sleep from about five in the afternoon until ten at night, but it drizzled much of the time and so we usually gave up and got on the move at about eight.

Then, on the second night at about 3 am, as we were drinking from the public well in a tiny village square, a guard from the Landwacht – Home Guard – appeared out of a dark doorway. Rather unwisely, thinking no one was about, we had been talking. The guard must have heard our foreign voices as he stood in the shadows. '*Halt!*' he shouted at us, blowing a whistle.

This was no time to practise my German. We ran, and he followed. But he was an old man and we soon left him behind as we reached open fields outside the village. Half an hour later we stopped running and crawled into a huge haystack just off the road.

Then took place an incident that was so extraordinary that David and I have never been able, properly, to explain it. It happened this way:

Dead tired, we were soon asleep in our haystack. We wakened with a start when we heard English voices close by. We peered out through the hay.

There, standing in a group and clearly visible by the light of early dawn, were the three officers who had left the cattle truck just after us. They stood there talking in loud voices. We got out to confront them. They were Ian Howie, Waddy Wadeson and Peter Griffiths.

93

'For God's sake, what are you doing?' David whispered. 'Someone will hear you. Clear off or they'll be after us. And shut up!'

'We'll join up with you,' one of them offered. 'We can all rest up in the haystack and move on together.'

We were furious.

'You bloody well won't! Get out – get moving!' David was using his most intimidating manner. The little group drifted off in the half light and disappeared.

The strange thing was, they had never been there at all.

Months later in a prison where we all found ourselves after recapture, we asked them why they had done such a rash thing, risking capture for all of us.

They didn't understand. They had never met up with us after the cattle truck, they said, nor could they have, as they had gone towards Switzerland on the opposite – the north side – of the river Inn. They looked at us as if we were mad. David and I said no more. We were quite shaken by what had been told to us.

If only one of us had had the experience it could be put down to a dream. But not only had we both had the same vision, but we had heard each other talk to the intruders, and heard their replies. In every respect it was real for both of us, and we agreed on every detail.

We have often talked about this strange event, but have never been able to explain it. Perhaps lack of sleep and hunger had brought on a joint hallucination with a telepathic element due to the nearness of the others on the far side of the river. Whatever the explanation, it was an uncanny experience.

Our encounter with the Landwacht meant that we could no longer travel by road at night. All other villages along the line would certainly have been alerted, and our march would now be restricted to the Alpine slopes by day. So we climbed wearily into the hills to start our trek.

That day was uneventful except that we had to wade through innumerable small streams flowing down the Alps into the Inn. By nightfall, we were wet, tired and very hungry. We slept fitfully, getting up to start as soon as it was light.

Around 2 pm we approached a small river and looking at it from the concealment of a wood, we saw that it had to be crossed by a wooden bridge. As bridges were often guarded, we watched for some time to see if there was any movement near by. There wasn't, and we walked down to cross it.

As we reached the far side of the bridge two Landwacht rose from their hiding place under it, rifles levelling at us. There was no place to run to.

We were marched down the slopes into the town of Landeck and, with little ado, shut up in cells.

For my part, I was too tired to care where I was. A dry cell with a board to sleep on seemed good enough at that point.

Next morning we were taken by train back to Innsbruck. It took half an hour. We had taken three days going that distance on foot in the other direction.

'Where are we going now?' I asked the guard at Innsbruck station where we were made to wait on a platform bench.

'To a big camp for Russian prisoners of war,' was the rather surprising reply.

'My Russian is a bit weak,' David remarked.

The joke fell flat as we knew that life was really tough for Russian prisoners, whom the Germans regarded as *Untermenschen*. In fact we felt distinctly apprehensive as we had no means of identification.

Another train trip brought us within an hour to a station where the sign read Markt Pongau.

One of the guards made a heavy joke. 'You can go skiing near by at Kitzbuhel,' he said. 'There are good hotels there.' So that was where we were. At least we knew where Kitzbuhel was.

As we were led in through the main gates we could see that it was a huge place. Hundreds of Russians in ragged green uniforms were walking about or sitting on the ground in groups. In the distance, about a quarter of a mile away, we saw a river that ran along the far side of the camp, the Pongau River.

We wondered what would happen next. We were lucky. We were taken to a wooden hut in a small compound right on the river. A Feldwebel opened the gate and let us in. There we found half a dozen of our friends from Gavi who, like ourselves, had got off the train at Innsbruck, but who had been captured earlier.

Among them was Mark Ogilvie Grant. He had painted murals with me two years ago at my first stop at Mont Albo near Piacenza.

'This is not a bad place and you'll find that they have accepted that we are English,' Mark told us. 'Every day we go to the hospital and a very nice German doctor gives us some extra food. Also, the hut is quite warm.'

It was warm but not luxurious, as eight of us lived in a room about twenty feet square. For several hours every morning, we were let out into a little yard to exercise. The yard had barbed wire seven feet high on the river side, and was separated by more wire on the three sides from the main Russian area. The Germans did not waste time disciplining the Russians. In the first place they took the view that peasant soldiers from the Urals or the Ukraine would have their work cut out getting home from any territory of the Third Reich. Moreover, Russian life was cheap. If a Russian stepped out of line, the guards merely shot him.

Mark was always good company and was light-hearted and dismissive of our plight. Somehow he had go hold of a French beret, greatcoat and sabots, and in this exotic dress he added tone to our forlorn little group. Moreover he had been in the compound for a week and knew the ropes.

'They don't pay much attention to us here,' he explained. 'The guard that stands at the gate mostly looks the other way into the Russian area. You'll be able to get out of here. A bit of patience, that's all you need,' he added consolingly.

It was clear that the only way out would be over the seven-foot barbed wire fence that ran along the river. On that side there were platforms with machine guns at one-hundred-yard intervals for as far as we could see in either direction. So we were under direct surveillance from these platforms and chances were not good.

Then one morning we found that mist was so thick in the yard that visibility was barely fifteen feet. David and I reckoned that we could not possibly be seen if we could get over the wire. We hurriedly discussed this with Mark. Mark loved trouble.

'It's easy,' he said. 'Get a blanket, throw it over the wire to cover the barbs, stand on my shoulders and you're away.' He was almost as pleased at the thought of this break as we were.

But even as we talked the mist was rising so we moved fast. All went well. Mark was a talented collaborator, and ten minutes later we were over the wire and standing on the river bank. The mist continued to rise at an alarming rate.

The break had come so unexpectedly that we had to pause for a moment to decide what to do next. But the rising mist decided for us: we would have to swim the river before we were spotted by guards in the machine-gun towers. We walked into the deep stream fully clothed with heavy boots on and struck out for the opposite bank.

I am a strong swimmer, and was not concerned about the fifty-yard swim. But almost at once a wave, breaking off an exposed boulder, hit me in the face and I took in a lungful of water. I could not get my breath and started to founder. I could see that David was all right ahead of me, but the rapid current was now sweeping us downstream past the machine guns which had free shots at us as we drifted past them. For my part I was in too great distress to notice the bullets hitting the water around me.

I managed to keep swimming, but soon went down for the second time. As I came up I knew I hadn't much left in me. I saw David reach the far bank – I wasn't far away and managed to keep swimming but very weakly. Suddenly my boots struck the bottom. I stood up in two feet of water. The fact was that I need not have swum for those last minutes when my strength was failing me.

But I was finished, and collapsed on the bank, my head in the high grass.

'We've got to keep going,' David exhorted me.

'I can't,' I gasped. 'I have to wait – I can't get up or move.'

At that moment we heard the barking of dogs. Looking upstream, about a quarter of a mile away on our side of the river, we could see through the thinning mist two soldiers running towards us with tracking dogs.

I got to my feet. 'Let's go,' I said.

We ran towards what looked to us like perpendicular wooded hills. The barking was very close behind us. I was in fact at the end of my strength, and only the baying of the dogs kept me going. We climbed up through the light undergrowth, David moving ahead of me with huge strides. The dogs were gaining on us, or so it sounded from the nearness of their barking. Finally my stomach revolted and I had to stop and be sick. This saved us, because, as we climbed higher and higher, we heard the barking suddenly stop. The dogs had clearly found something more interesting than our tracks.

This respite took us out of reach of our pursuers and by night-time we were high in the Alps out of range of the Germans. We found a haystack; crawled into it and went to sleep.

We walked all the next day and the day after, traversing a spine of mountains running east. We had no plan: Jugoslavia was to the east and we vaguely aimed for there. We were on a sure loser, but we were free and on our own. That seemed worth while.

On the second night just before dusk we saw below us on the alpine slope a farm cottage with lights. The cottage was so isolated that I felt we could go and ask for food without much danger.

We descended towards the lights, and arrived at the little house unheralded by any dogs. Looking through the window into the big farm kitchen we saw a young woman at the stove and a man with his back to us, sitting at a table.

I knocked at the door which was answered by the man. We were Italians, I said, trying to get to Markt Pongau and from there back to Italy to fight the British. Where was the road to Markt Pongau? I asked. It was an unlikely story, but the man invited us in.

His wife, a smiling and typical young Austrian hausfrau, asked if we would like some of the soup she was cooking and I said we would. She gave us a huge bowlful, and bread to go with it. We were ravenous.

We talked about the war. I told them that David knew no German, only Italian. This left him free to devote himself to the soup. We agreed that the Italian capitulation was terrible, and the importance of loyal Italians sticking with their old allies. I also asked some guarded questions as to where we were, and what was the next town to the east.

After a while the husband rose to his feet, put on his coat and left. He had chores to do with the cows in the barn, and the goats had to be brought in.

I chatted with his wife. She had a tick in her left eye, but was a warm and friendly character. After the soup, she brought up cheese and hot milk. We had really fallen on our feet, and felt warm and well fed for the first time in weeks. Warmed by a roaring fire half an hour passed quickly.

Suddenly the door opened and the husband appeared with four Landwacht. He had walked down into the valley to fetch them while we were eating. His wife did not have a tick in her eye: she was on our side and was encouraging us to get out. Obviously she had not dared to talk for fear her husband was listening at the door. She looked sad as we were led off. She must have liked us. We were furious with ourselves for not picking up her tip-off.

After a night in the local police station we were taken back to the Russian camp, and two days later were put on a train and told we were going to Berlin for interrogation. We were quite unable to figure out why we should be taken nearly five hundred miles for interrogation. Interrogation about what?

*

The train was a slow one and stopped at practically every station. In our carriage were a crowd of Russian women – all soldiers and all prisoners of war. A few of them spoke a little German. They said they had been told they were going to a concentration camp to be shot for partisan activities. They seemed unconcerned, their flat Slav features quite impassive.

Eventually we were told to get out. We were at Lückenwalde, just outside Berlin, and were marched from the station to a camp with impressive illuminated barbed wire around it, and guard dog patrols everywhere. The guards were SS men – not a good omen.

We entered a building where we were locked into a small room for half an hour, after which a British sergeant entered. He said he had a job as interpreter and started to ask us a lot of questions about where we came from. According to him he had the guards under control – he was a 'trusty', he said, and would help us get plenty to eat. He questioned us in much detail. We had been very persistent in escaping, the German commandant had told him. He hoped it was because we were set on sabotage. Was it? We laughed and told him that our only objective was to escape and get back to England. What would we sabotage? We not only had no explosives, but were also practically starved.

Soon it became clear that our 'British' sergeant was a stool pigeon. His questions were altogether too professional to arise from ordinary curiosity. Moreover, we detected a slight Dublin accent. It gradually became clear he was an Irish renegade, and, realizing this, we insisted more and more on the fact that we were ordinary British officers doing their duty in escaping. What on earth had we been brought to this interrogation centre for?

After about an hour, the sergeant left and we were taken by an SS man and lodged in separate cells next to each other. On the way we agreed that at all costs we must disprove the suspicion that we were saboteurs. Saboteurs got short shrift from the Germans.

There was no need. Our sergeant must have reported that we were harmless escapers, because at dawn next day we were awoken, given a breakfast of soup and black bread and marched off to the railway station. With us were some newcomers – all had been questioned by the sergeant about sabotage: none were saboteurs but simply escapers like ourselves. Our guards told us we were going south, back to where we had just come from; and next day we arrived at Eichstätt north of Nürnberg in Bavaria.

Eichstätt was the camp where almost all the officers captured at Dunkirk, Calais, and 'Boulogne were imprisoned. As it had been in existence for three years it was properly organized. The officers received Red Cross parcels of food, clothes from their families, and regular mail. After the events of the past three months, we were ready for the dull, institutionalized life of this established camp.

What was not institutional about Eichstätt was the attitude of the prisoners towards their German captors.

Dunkirk rankled. These officers felt the full frustration of having in many cases gone straight from English bases into the bag in the matter of weeks. Their hatred of Germans responsible for their plight evidenced itself in resisting the German prison authorities in every way they could. In effect they tried to continue the war in microcosm inside the camp using disrespect and mockery as weapons.

This they did in a variety of ways. They refused to salute German superior officers. They relentlessly imitated and mocked the guards. They refused to treat roll calls as the formal parade that the Germans would have liked. When the Germans shouted, 'Attention!' everyone turned to talk to his neighbour, or continued reading a book. When ordered to dismiss by the German taking the parade, the British Officers lounged about, but came to attention when the Senior British officer ordered 'Dismiss'. They would then turn smartly to the right and march off. The Germans hated this unruly behaviour, and it was perhaps somewhat childish; but it helped to work out the frustration that they all felt.

Before our first morning's roll call David and I were each given a pair of handcuffs, and told to put them on before parading. This was a real surprise, but an explanation was forthcoming.

Apparently after some commando raid in Northern France, a platoon of Germans had been captured and handcuffed before being taken back by submarine to England. As a reprisal all officers at Eichstätt were to wear handcuffs during the hours of daylight. That was the order; but that is not what happened.

Before roll call officers clipped on their handcuffs and stayed that way until dismissed. Then, using implements made from kitchen utensils, everyone unlocked their handcuffs, slung them over their shoulders and returned to their huts. This procedure had been going on for several months before our arrival, and had

101

in the first instance evoked all sorts of punishment. But as no punishment had any effect, the Germans gave up and settled for a roll call with handcuffs and nothing more. Dumb insolence is very hard to compete with.

The activities of the last two months now told on me, and I was put into hospital with a strained heart and a murmur. There I spent the Christmas of 1943, warm and better fed than the others. I was recovering and feeling better by mid January when David came in one evening and told me that eighty officers including ourselves were moving next day to a new camp in Czechoslovakia on the borders of Poland. I got out of pyjamas and into uniform to take the train; and after a slow trip in heavy snow we arrived at our destination late at night and got out onto the station platform. 'Märisch Trübau' read the station sign.

CHAPTER SIX

Märisch Trübau, Moravia – Part One

Cold moonlight lit the streets of this old Sudeten–Czech town as we were marched through the snowy streets to our new camp, not far from Austerlitz, scene of Napoleon's great victory over the Russians in 1805. It was stimulating to think that we were out of Germany itself, in Czechoslovakia, scene of one of Germany's first aggressions in central Europe.

This new camp was on a slope, with the town below and a thick pinewood above. At one time the Czech military academy, its lay-out made it better adapted to housing prisoners than most of the places I had been in. An enormous wooden building which we called the Biscuit Factory was the central complex, and it was surrounded by thirteen satellite wooden barracks and several large games fields. It was nearly a mile around, enclosed by two rings of barbed wire about ten feet apart, and guarded by sentry towers placed at regular and rather close intervals.

We were greeted by Alastair Cram. After leaving us at the train at Mezza Coronna in Northern Italy, he told us he had travelled east with great difficulty by goods train, and had eventually been recaptured near Graz in Styria. The Gestapo had given him a bad time, but in the end had sent him to Märisch Trübau. Apparently most of the POWs that had made escapes during the chaos that followed the Italian capitulation had been herded here. The record of the Gavi contingent during the move was spectacular. Out of 180 officers there had been 100 attempted escapes; three were killed escaping; fifteen reached Jugoslavia; and about a dozen were safe in Switzerland. It had been an expensive move for the Germans.

We walked all arund the camp and talked to old friends who

had been there for a few months. The situation seemed to be pretty clear. The camp was so spread out and the embryo German organization so loose, that chances of getting out looked remarkably good. Moreover, we were on the doorstep of a country that was pro-Allied and it was reasonable to expect that help would be offered to anyone on the run. Looking around us on the first day, the place looked like a gift for the determined escaper. On the British side there was as yet no proper organization or hierarchy of authority to control the adventurous officer. The Senior British Officer, Colonel Waddilove, was doing his best to get the 3,000 British POWs under some sort of discipline, but we could see that he was having a hard time.

Personally, I expected to get out pretty quickly.

'I don't think we'll be here for long,' I said to David. 'With Poland close by on one side and the Protectorate on the other, we have friends at hand for once. It should only be a question of getting out and finding help to move us on further, or,' I said as an afterthought, 'we could get out and simply stay put among friendly people until it's all over.'

'Exactly what I have been thinking, but I've got a better idea. Why not turn the whole camp into one big escape organization? Right now the place is pretty chaotic and there should be a good chance of orienting it on new lines before it settles down into the usual rut.'

I was taken aback by this idea. In some ways it was as unique as the original concept of the SAS; but functioning under the vigilance of a prison would be vastly different from bulldozing through the prejudices of orthodox generals in the Middle East.

'You've got no chance,' I said. 'No one will accept that kind of regimentation.'

I had been a prisoner for longer than David, and I knew perhaps better than he how strongly individualistic prisoners became. They tended to resent any restraint on what little independence their lives offered. In short, they didn't like to be told what to do.

'Assuming it's possible,' I said, 'how are you going to go about it?'

Märisch Trübau, Moravia – Part One

'Well, first of all by convincing the SBO that it is a worthwhile idea. If I can get his agreement to that, then we will have to do a selling operation right through the camp. My idea is to organize an operation that would get about 150 officers free. That's 5% of the camp. Then enlist all the others to help in ways we would have to devise and explain. For one thing, it would have the effect of motivating the whole population of the camp in one direction. The majority who wouldn't be in on the escape would at least have a feeling that they were part of something and were making a contribution. I have a feeling it might work.'

'Let's try it,' I said.

David went off to see Colonel Waddilove, a charming and very approachable man who had been captured on the island of Kos. We had formulated a scheme to put before him. David thought it would have so many attractions that he would be able to get agreement for the plan.

The proposal was for David to originate, control and co-ordinate all escape activities. No individual efforts of any kind to be allowed. Such a thing was unheard of, but David set out to sell the idea to the SBO. He was a talented persuader who did not always convince by logic, rather by giving the strong impression that he was sorry for you if you were not up to grasping his point. The SBO was attracted by the idea. At first he didn't think it was feasible, but he was made an offer that he could hardly refuse: in return for carte blanche to organize the whole camp as an escape organization, David undertook to obtain a wireless set with which to listen to the BBC, to organize security measures in the camp, and to provide an intelligence service that would keep the camp informed of the political and military situation around us. This was an attractive offer and the SBO agreed. In fact when David made these promises he had no idea how he would be able to keep them. David was not short of self-confidence.

We got to work quickly, knowing that we had a really first-class nucleus of experienced and trustworthy people from the Italian camps, especially from Gavi, who would rally to the cause.

All this had been agreed when I came down with pneumonia and was hospitalized for ten days and out of action.

During this time a lot happened. David had organized two rooms in one of the barrack huts exclusively for us so that we would have total privacy. We asked Mark Ogilvie Grant if he would come in with us as a backroom boy and do our cooking. He agreed. We were very lucky to have him along. Mark contributed a light-hearted humour that was a great blessing, as the activities of David and myself were a bit heavy, concentrated as they were on the grand escape plan. He was utterly secure and never mentioned how boring we must have been to live with. Getting up in the morning, freezing cold, Mark would don his French officer's greatcoat and wooden sabots. Then he would set about boiling water on our stove for the ersatz coffee and cut our wafer-thin slices of rationed bread. Usually he sang his favourite song:

> Dear Auntie Nellie's
> Great bouncing jellies
> *How* they delight all the men!

Morale at the start of a gloomy day was often boosted by these merry sounds. He also added tone to the establishment by painting gnomes, fairies and forest animals all over the walls.

By the end of January 1944 we were under way with the organization. David headed it; I was his deputy.

There were four sections. The first was intelligence, which I ran. I will describe this section later. Of the others, the most important was security.

Here we were fortunate in finding an officer of quite exceptional ability to head it. Anthony Simkins, about thirty, but looking more like twenty, had been a promising barrister before the war, had joined the Rifle Brigade, but had been captured very early in the desert. His was a clear, incisive intellect, and he had an exceptional ability to quickly separate the important from the unimportant. David and I were not surprised that in later life he became Deputy Director General of MI5. His work at Märisch Trübau must have whetted his appetite for this type of work – anyway, this is what he says, indicating that we were talent-spotters.

Anthony appointed a deputy security officer in each of the thirteen barracks and two in the Biscuit Factory. If we were to run an escape organization of this magnitude then security would be of paramount importance. All sorts of small things can happen in prison life which might give information to the prison staff. For instance, a prisoner, talking to a guard, might mention the capture of such and such a place – perhaps by the Russians perhaps by the Germans. This place may not have been mentioned in the German communiqués, and an alert guard would report the conversation. The implication would be that we had heard this news on the BBC: that we had a radio in other words. Searches would follow. This is only one example of the many aspects of security that Anthony watched for and that his deputies checked on continuously, reporting to him every day.

The next section was the news agency. This was run by a Palestinian Jew, Ben Aharon by name. Ben originally came from Central Europe and had a wide knowledge of its recent political history. He had an academic background and an intimate knowledge of Germany – an ideal person in fact to run the agency.

The agency was a two-faced affair. Officially it distributed the legitimately bought German newspapers, putting out translations of the most interesting articles, even openly maintaining an office in the Biscuit Factory with a staff of German speakers. Sub rosa, however, it received and edited the BBC news and other foreign broadcasts for verbal retailing throughout the camp by security officers. It was this BBC news that nourished the camp's morale.

Our radio – acquisition of which satisfied one of David's commitments to the SBO – was acquired through a young Czech carpenter employed on maintenance work in the camp who became a great friend to us. We had given him some gold coins to buy it with, and with great risk to himself he had gone to Prague and obtained one.

The radio was in the charge of 'Porky' Gowan, a regular officer captured in Norway who had run the radio at Eichstätt. He lived in a room with two others each of whom was tri-lingual in English, French and German. Between them they picked up all interesting broadcasts. The radio was kept in a hide under the floorboards of his room. This hide was in two parts: pressure on a nail opened a trap door that covered a first cavity where we stored some maps and compasses. These were meant to satisfy the Germans if they ever discovered the hide. But inside this compartment pressure on another nail dislodged a concrete block behind which the radio was kept. From eight until midnight Porky and his two colleagues operated their set, and next day news was distributed throughout the camp.

The third section was the police force and manpower pool. This was a bright idea of David's, and it performed a very necessary function in view of the size of the escape operation we planned. John Newman, a major in the South African Army, ran this section with a force of about two hundred volunteers. They varied in rank from brigadier to subaltern.

This force had two functions. The first was to keep track of every German who entered the camp. To do this a flying squad hung around the main gate all day observing the comings and goings of the prison staff. Every German when he entered would be followed until he left by a detachment of the flying squad who operated in pairs. One man tailed the German; the other would act as runner and report back to Newman exactly where he was and what he was doing until he left.

The second function was to supply stooges to guard those working on the various aspects of escape: tunnelling, making hides or maps and compasses, and document forging. Newman's men had full responsibility for safeguarding those at work on our projects. It was not an easy task, and to avoid attracting attention these stooges often went to ingenious lengths. I remember seeing a colonel sitting out in deep snow and freezing weather with an easel in front of him ostensibly painting a picture of the hideous Biscuit Factory. In fact he was keeping watch outside the radio hut where repairs were going on with the set. Newman devised many such ruses, and ran his section with very strict discipline, something which only a strong, attractive personality could enforce on a prisoner.

These then were the officers running security, news and the

police. Before describing the intelligence branch which I ran myself it will be worth looking at David's overall concept which gave the organization, and particularly the intelligence branch, its orientation.

David intended to get about 150 officers out of the camp into Czechoslovakia by June 1944. We hoped, by then, that the invasion of the continent would have taken place and the German grip on Europe would have weakened. In order to make it possible for such a large number of escapees to stay free inside search cordons that would inevitably be thrown out, it would be necessary for each selected man to have detailed briefing on local conditions. For them, at this stage of the war, with security measures inside the Reich tightening every day, haphazard knowledge of conditions would not be sufficient.

The first object of the intelligence, therefore, was to build up the best possible information on local conditions, terrain, railways and communications, in order to enable the escapist to have a sporting chance, based on reasonably good knowledge of what he was up against.

Our second object, of prime importance, and one which only our proximity to the Protectorate made possible was to contact the Czech Underground. This was the Obrana Naroda started before the war by Frantisek Moraveć.

Thirdly we wanted to establish liaison with friendly locals in case the war suddenly came to an end. We were in a tight corner with the frontiers of Poland, Germany and Slovakia only miles away. It was possible that when the confusion of war overtook these territories, traditional enemies might start quarrelling and perhaps liquidate each other. In this case, we were in the middle.

These were the demands on the intelligence branch which I ran. To cope with the demands, I broke intelligence down into three sections.

The first section had the task of developing a relationship with local people sympathetic to us, starting with the German, Czech and Sudeten workmen who came into the camp every day on maintenance work, usually without any guard in attendance.

To handle this delicate and somewhat risky work, I chose Ian

109

Howie who had been at Gavi. He was a sophisticated person, spoke good German and Italian, and had a disarming manner. Tall, lanky and with a facade of friendliness that was very convincing, he managed to give the impression that he was completely impartial. Listening to him chatting to guards, you could believe that he saw the German point of view, the Czech point of view, the Polish point of view, the Allied point of view, all depending on who was with him. In truth he was a 'man for all seasons'.

Howie recruited his own German speakers, and each one became 'the Minder' of one of the artisans. They disposed of cigarettes, coffee and chocolate that the SBO kept back from our Red Cross parcels for this express purpose. The Minders developed a 'cupboard love' relationship with their subjects. It was a relationship which brought us a great deal of local information and resulted in several of the workmen actually undertaking tasks in the outside world, that we, on the inside, could not possibly have done.

Jack White-Abbott, originally an intelligence staff officer, ran the section that culled information about our surrounding world. He organized and supervised the interrogation of officers with pre-war travel experience in these areas, and he documented the information he obtained. For instance, a man who had once travelled from Vienna to Prague by rail would have his memory ransacked to describe the stations he had gone through en route and the terrain he had passed through. If he had made a stop, he would be asked to describe the station where the ticket office was, the lavatory, provost marshal's office, at least as well as could be remembered.

In this way, by interrogation of dozens of officers and by the questioning of Ian Howie's artisan 'friends', we were able to build up dossiers of information with which to brief officers volunteering for the break. This information covered Poland, Hungary, Austria, Germany, and the Protectorate itself. Once collected, it was collated and drawn up in a syllabus oriented to escape purposes. Six briefers took groups of intending escapers in instruction on all aspects dealing with their route and plans. An escaping prisoner is often recaptured (if not because of hunger or fatigue) then because he has to make a quick decision in an emergency and lacks local knowledge to make the right one. We wanted to make sure that no one got caught through lack of knowledge that could possibly be obtained for him in advance.

Secure hides for escape paraphernalia had high priority. It was impossible to run an exercise of this magnitude without storing up maps, documents and food for the hundred and fifty escapers. To overcome this problem David recruited a team of four experts – an engineer, architect and two cabinet makers – whose task it was to build precision hides, and to devise concealment for escape projects. They worked with a few improvised tools, but the work they did and the ingenious concealment of hides that they achieved was astounding.

Finally in order that all information of whatever nature that came into the camps could find its way to the relevant quarter, David set up a clearing house which met every day and over which I presided. It was a kind of 'Think Tank'. Those attending were Simkins (Security); Aharon and Gowan (BBC and newspapers); White-Abbott (de-briefing), and Howie (local contacts).

At these meetings everything we had learnt that day from the radio, from newspapers, or from our informers was discussed and the significance assessed with reference not only to our escape plans but to the predicament of the camp generally. Knowledge of the sentiment and attitude of the locals was of special interest. Information of this nature was reported to the SBO who, as in most camps, had drawn up detailed military plans which would take effect if events made it necessary for the camp to fend for itself in a confused military situation.

Important work was meanwhile being carried out by forgers and map-makers, under the direction of Pat Clayton. Clayton was a brilliant cartographer and draughtsman. He had in fact made most of the maps of the Western desert. Under his supervision maps, passports, ration cards, identity cards, railway tickets – all were forged and were wellnigh indistinguishable from the originals. The originals from which he worked were obtained by Ian Howie's gang who would 'borrow' them for a few hours from their contacts and return them.

Compasses were improvised in large numbers from razor blades, and dozens of German uniforms and civilian suits were made up out of grey issued blankets by a team of expert seamsters whom Yves St Laurent would have been lucky to employ ten years later.

By early March work on all these requisites for escape was proceeding apace and on a large scale. Everyone actively helping was promised a place in the big break designed to give him his freedom. Many officers volunteered their help but did not claim a place on the escape. They were ready to contribute without reward.

While these background activities were being inched forward, five enterprises had been started.

The first was called 'Enterprise X'. This was an underground compartment in the SBO's hut with an ingenious entrance under a stone slab in the bathroom floor. Work on this went on uninterrupted with the object of enlarging it to dimensions able to accommodate a substantial party of escapers who could tunnel from there.

Then a hide had to be constructed in the roof of one of the buildings for storage of supplies on a grand scale. This was necessary as it was envisaged that we would need rations for a hundred and fifty escapers.

Three tunnels were also started, each run by leader responsible for organizing the work and for reporting back to David on their progress. Newman's men looked after the workers' security. All three started from under barrack-room floors and were driven in the direction of the wire, usually a distance of under thirty feet. Unfortunately, all three tunnels started to flood. There was no hope of saving them. To make the best of it, we passed on an anonymous note to a German guard disclosing their locations. This note purported to come from a religious fanatic who did not want to see life squandered in this reckless way. He promised to inform on any further escaping projects as well. We hoped that this might induce the Germans to let up on their overall vigilance. But it was only making the best of a bad job.

The main escape route, aimed at giving a hundred and fifty officers their freedom, was the 'Wire Job'.

This was David's own idea. Having convinced the Germans that the Scottish officers needed a 'Highland Dancing Platform' (whatever that may mean), and having procured the necessary wood to build it, David got a civil engineer and a team of amateur carpenters to construct a series of ten trestle bridges, each twenty feet long by three feet wide, reinforced with tin from the Red Cross parcels. These would be able, when laid from one stable point to another, to support fifteen men each. Until the escape, they would lie side by side en bloc, on the auditorium floor, disguised as our Highland Dancing Platform. When German guards were around, half a dozen officers would have a go at dancing on the platform – a rather bizarre sight.

The plan depended on achieving total surprise, and of neutralizing the guards during the time the escape was taking place. This was to be done by fusing all lights and drenching the machine-gun posts with water. Howie arranged this through his contacts, who procured the hoses. They also volunteered when the time came, to operate the fuse box, the location of which was unguarded in the German area outside.

Looking back it is clear that the operation was dangerous, not so much in the escape formula itself, but in the reaction the Germans were likely to have afterwards. We thought that the worst that would happen to anyone would be re-capture and some routine punishment. We did not know what became clear later on, namely that the Germans would almost certainly regard such a mass escape as an enemy uprising. Uprisings of this nature, especially in occupied territories, were ruthlessly dealt with by the SS. There would have been few survivors amongst those recaptured. But none of this was obvious at the time, when the extreme measures of Himmler, introduced to protect the Reich, had only just started to bite.

As far as we knew, nothing like this had ever been attempted from a prison camp before.

But first we wanted to ensure that the reconnaissance party itself had contacts to go to when the time came for them to get out.

This was arranged by Ian Howie, who succeeded in getting five of the workmen to agree to take one escaper each into his house in the Protectorate. Each member of the mission would carry with him a list of questions to answer. We in turn would receive their answers from our friend the Czech carpenter to whose house in Prague all communication would be addressed. He went home every weekend and could collect the letters and bring them to us on his return to Märisch Trübau.

For this mission experienced escapers all speaking good German were chosen. They were: Ian Howie, Waddy Wadeson, a balding mining engineer of about fifty; Hugh McKenzie, a much-escaped Seaforth Highlander; Peter Griffiths, a South African who had been at Gavi; and Leslie Hill, ex-Cambridge student, who spoke a dozen languages and possessed a photographic memory.

During March, these five underwent a special course of training. They learnt basic Czech from a Czech officer captured with the British Army; they learnt from intelligence officers how to act under interrogation; they planned their stories with me and got documents from Pat Clayton's forgery factory to back them up; and they walked and jogged ten miles a day around the compound.

*

At the same time, with our eyes on the objective of contacting the Czech Underground, David and I became interested in one Captain Van Zouco, a doctor working in the camp and professing to be a South African officer. He apparently boasted that he was in the confidence of the Germans. Anthony Simkins had spotted that his past history was suspect and no one could figure out why he had turned up at Märisch Trübau. David asked me to investigate.

I went around to the hospital and found Van Zouco sitting in his room with the German welfare officer, Dr Ackerman. As I came in I noticed that he was talking German with no trace of an accent and drinking a glass of schnapps. Seeing me enter, Ackerman rose, exchanged a few pleasantries and left.

'My name is Pringle,' I said to Van Zouco, 'and I have come along from Stirling because we hear you have some German contacts and get interesting confidences out of them. Have they told you anything unusual lately?'

Van Zouco didn't reply but watched me closely. Then he poured me a drink. I studied him. He was obviously a Jew, about thirty-four, dark with a thin moustache, wavy black hair and a good-looking face in a smooth, oily way. He radiated a kind of magnetism.

'Of course, I know about you and Stirling,' he answered eventually, sitting back on his bed. He spoke English with a strong German accent. '*Ja*, I think I have heard something that will interest you. Ackerman, that bastard that just left the room – he told me that we have an informer in the camp. Those three tunnels they found – an informer told them. And another thing I . . .'

'Wait a minute, you say that the Germans were tipped off about the whereabouts of those tunnels.'

'*Ja*,' said Zouco. He always said '*Ja*' instead of 'Yes'. 'Ackerman just told me now.'

This was interesting, because David and I had indeed written an anonymous letter to the Germans, informing them of the whereabouts of the tunnels.

So Ackerman had at least told Van Zouco a partial truth of a confidential nature.

'Does Ackerman always talk freely with you or is he normally more careful?' I asked after a pause during which he poured me some more schnapps.

'Listen.' He got to his feet and spoke with the self-confidence that I later learnt was part of his style. 'I can get anything from these Germans – anything! Do you want something? I get it for you. Tell me what you and Stirling want – I get it!'

'That's a liberal offer,' I suggested. He ignored my tone.

'It's more than liberal, it's bloody well true! and I prove it to you! You just give me the chance, ask me for something, and I get it. I *get* it!' He was quite excited by this time and had got hold of a button on my battledress which he was twisting.

I got up and finished the drink.

'Look,' I said, 'don't come around to our rooms unless I send for you. I don't want the Germans to notice you coming to see us. But I'll tell Stirling what you've told me – we'll probably want to talk to you again later. Meanwhile, let me know if you hear anything else interesting. Thank you for the schnapps.'

'Listen!' He crowded close up to me as I stood with my hand on the door knob. 'I'd be bloody happy to be in on this party. Tell Stirling I want to help, and I *can* help too, believe me!'

When I got back to the room, David and Mark were frying some bread for supper on our rickety little stove.

'What happened?' asked David.

I told about my meeting and added that I was impressed, first by his quick wits and, secondly, by the slippery impression he gave.

'Certainly sounds suspicious. All the same, he did tell you what is perfectly true and what only five people in the camp know: that three tunnels had been tipped off by an informer's letter. You can't get around that.'

'It seems to me,' I said, 'that even if we can't trust him on our present knowledge of his dossier, we can use him to get us some of the things we need. That is, if he is as good at getting around the Germans as he says he is. If we don't tell him anything and just use him, we can't lose anything.'

'It's risky, and there's a lot at stake – but I agree. Get him up here this evening and we'll give him something simple for a start and if he delivers the goods we'll give him some really interesting ones to break his teeth on. But we'll treat him, from all security points of view, as if he were a German until we know more about him.' Anthony Simkins had insisted on this.

Later that evening Van Zouco came in. Good judge of atmosphere and mood that he was, he adopted an attitude of respect for David, didn't talk too much, and showed no curiosity about our plans. He said he was Belgian, had been at Berlin University studying medicine before the war, and had then been put in a concentration camp as a Jew. He escaped to Brussels so he said and had joined up with the South African medical service when the war started. Now what he wanted was some way to help the British cause. I was doing no talking and had a good opportunity of watching him. He seemed certain of himself, respectful but not obsequious, but when David talked to him or questioned him, he was hard to pin down to facts. He often tried to evade a question by volunteering an alternative bit of information. He was obviously anxious to be believed and uncertain as to whether he would be.

'Well,' said David eventually, 'the first thing we want you to do is to get us a spare wireless valve. Secondly, when you go to the German hospital at Zwittau (a nearby town in Czechoslovakia) with the next bunch of POWs for the medical examination before repatriation – Jack Pringle is one of them – see that he has as much freedom of movement as possible. Can you do this?'

'You bet I can, Colonel.' Van Zouco was smiling delightedly. 'You just leave it to me.'

I should mention here that my bout of pneumonia had aggravated the murmurs in my heart, and I was to go before a German medical board for a repatriation report. Van Zouco accompanied all candidates for repatriation to the German hospital at Zwittau, and supervised their stay there. We had decided that the Zwittau trips provided the best and probably the only opportunity for me to make contact with the Czech Underground. It was important that we should have definite information and specific contacts with the Underground before the special mission went out. It had to be done by me, as only David and I knew all the angles of the operation, and David couldn't speak German.

Next week, early in April, surrounded by guards, a small party of ten of us, plus Van Zouco as doctor-in-charge, set off by local train for Zwittau. It didn't take me long to notice that Van Zouco had the guard Feldwebel eating out of his hand, and his talk with him had the tone of master and man rather than prisoner and guard. I later came to recognize this as Van Zouco's usual method of dealing with Germans.

Arrived at the hospital, he somehow got me into a small private cubicle, guarded by an amiable Bavarian soldier to whom I gave presents of chocolate and coffee. In a short while, we were talking about his native Bavaria and he had pictures of his wife and three wooden-looking children out on the table. Inside half an hour we had a working agreement not to bother one another. I told him I was too sick to want to escape and he said that as long as I didn't escape he didn't care what I did as long as the Feldwebel didn't see.

Pretty soon, Van Zouco came along with a pretty Czech nurse. It was about five in the evening on that first day.

'Fräulein,' he said. 'let me introduce my best friend, Major Count Pringle. This is Sister Gerda.'

My surprise at being promoted to best friend and count all at once was nearly too much for me to disguise.

Van Zouco continued blandly in English: 'Keep her in here, feed her chocolate and make friends. She will be useful and will be able to help you move around the hospital. I am going to see about getting that valve.' He pronounced it 'walw'. 'I am quite free here.'

It was no hardship to keep Gerda talking in the room for about half an hour. When she had overcome her shyness, she evinced great curiosity about life in England and I, on my part, asked her many questions about Sudetenland and Czechoslovakia, from much less disinterested motives. At about six o'clock I asked her if she would take me to the hospital chapel adjoining the hospital. Van Zouco had recommended me to have a look at it as soon as I could. She was quite willing and, together with the Bavarian guard, we went downstairs, through a large oak door and into the small adjoining Roman Catholic chapel. I was anxious to train my guard along the right lines, so, at the door, I told him that it was not necessary for him to accompany us. Rather to my surprise, he agreed, and Gerda and I went in alone, kneeling

118

down in the back row. Someone was playing the organ, and there were only a few worshippers in the church. I looked around me. It was an excellent place for a rendezvous; if there was any business to be done it could be done here.

Half an hour later, I was in the hospital kitchen with Gerda helping the cook to make supper for the other nine British officers in the main ward. These nine were in a large ward under proper guard. The cook was a jolly old thing, very anti-Nazi. The scullery maid was a sluttish Czech girl with pronounced Slav features. I was wondering what had happened to Van Zouco when he came in suddenly from the garden door with another nurse. He had lipstick on the side of his neck which I told him, in English, to wipe off.

'Sister Gizela,' he said, quite unabashed, turning to the nurse with him, 'may I present my best friend, Major Count Pringle, one of the biggest landowners in England.'

I bowed (as I thought one of the biggest landowners in England should bow). It didn't take me long to notice that Sister Gizela was infatuated with Van Zouco. Her eyes never left him and she showed clearly how much she disapproved of any attention he paid to Gerda. Van Zouco himself, who behaved like the complete master of hospital, nurses, guards, domestics and food, was in his element.

'I got out after supper,' he said to me in English, offering me half a fried chicken and a hardboiled egg from his overcoat pocket. 'You wait up for me until I get back – I got something bloody interesting for you. I got the walw too.'

This was not bad progress. I sat up talking to my guard until midnight. When Van Zouco came in we told him to leave us alone, which he did. Van Zouco was in high spirits.

'First the walw,' he said, and put it down on the table. 'Second thing was plenty of freedom for you. You got enough? It isn't the matter' – his phrase for 'it doesn't matter' – 'tomorrow will be better, next day better still. And that nurse Gizela – you know the one? My friend, she is half Polish and she hates these Germans worse than we do. She got the walw. She will help more too. You'll see. Now I must go. I got to meet Gizela half-past twelve.' He was gone.

As I climbed into bed, I thought over the events of the day. In spite of our unwillingness to trust Van Zouco, David had agreed before I left that if his performance warranted taking big risks, I was to take them. Thinking of it, it looked to me as if I were in a unique position for a British prisoner as closely guarded as myself. I had considerable freedom, no security supervision, no parole asked (no one ever gave parole) and in Van Zouco I had a contact man who was on friendly terms with the anti-Nazi element in the hospital. Van Zouco could be a stool pigeon, he could be from the Gestapo, but the main thing was that prisoners could not be choosers and he had already produced quite unusual results in the only two tasks allotted him. If he turned out to be Gestapo, it would be just too bad for me and David. It not, we might get information and make contacts otherwise quite out of the question for a prisoner. Before going to sleep, I decided to take the risk and ask Van Zouco to put me in touch with an agent of the Czech Underground, in the course of the next two days.

Next morning, I told Van Zouco what I wanted. I told him I wanted to meet personally with a member of the Czech Underground, and that my purpose in wanting to meet him would be to discuss the possibilities of getting help for prisoners in the event of a Nazi débâcle. This was the minimum confidence I could give him under the conditions. He said he'd do his best.

I didn't see him all that day as he was at doctors' conferences or anyway not in the ward. I toured fairly freely around the hospital, spent a couple of hours peeling potatoes with the scullery maid, another couple helping to clean the wards with Gerda, and the afternoon discussing the war with wounded German soldiers on the floor below. Best of all, my guard took me for a two-hour walk in the town, where I had a good chance to observe useful things such as prices of food, location of the railway and police stations, and I talked to locals in the café where we drank coffee. This semi-normal life was a great tonic after the routine of prison. In the late afternoon, I had my medical examination. Van Zouco did not turn up in my room until half past ten that night.

'It's fixed up,' he said, 'but believe me, my best fellow, it was not easy. Even now it will be bloody risky. I'll tell you what I've done.'

It appeared that he had gone to Gizela, and trading on her affection for him, asked her if she knew anyone, Pole or Czech, who had contact with the Underground and to whom she would introduce him. She said she did, but that the risks were too great on both sides. Her brother, who worked in the hospital office, didn't trust Van Zouco because he spoke German like a native. Van Zouco had then said that it was the British major (myself) for whom he wanted the contact and that it was I alone who would meet and talk with any contact she made. She still refused.

'Then,' said Van Zouco resignedly, as if this sort of thing had happened too often before, 'I took her up in the organ loft in the church. I told her I loved her and wanted to marry her after the war. I said please, please, if she wanted to help me and the Allies, do this one thing for me. In the end, she said she would give her own word to her brother that I was OK. She said if anything went wrong she would be shot. She is a nice girl,' added the romantic doctor, as an afterthought.

'Well?' I said.

'So she went to her brother, and bringed me along. He was not so bloody keen on this. But after I talked and tell him about you, he agrees to find out what his boss says. The brother is nothing – just a member – but there is someone in Zwittau who is pretty big. Before dinner her brother goes out, and when he comes back he says all right, someone will be here from Prague tomorrow. Meet you in the church at 2.30 in the afternoon. I fix it so you go there alone. Christ, I hope it's all right!'

Quite honestly, I was hoping so myself, because this kind of game would end in plenty of trouble if we were being double-crossed. I didn't sleep very well that night. There was a lot of room for error here. I could be double-crossed by Van Zouco. Van Zouco and I could be double-crossed by Gizela and her brother. And all of us could be caught if the Gestapo happened to be watching the man arriving from Prague. However, as I looked at it, we stood to gain so much that the risk had to be taken.

CHAPTER SEVEN

Märisch Trübau, Moravia – Part Two

When I woke up the next morning at seven, I found Oberleutnant Haberhauer, the Märisch Trübau Camp Security Officer standing at the bottom of my bed, gazing down at me through the thick lenses of his glasses. He had a slant-eyed Japanese look on his greasy fat face, and a cunning expression that did not belie the active brain behind it. Of all the people in Germany, he was the one I least wanted to see in that hospital, and I could not imagine what had brought him twenty miles at seven in the morning. I felt decidedly unhappy.

'Good morning, Herr Major,' he said. 'What a pity about your heart. *Eine grosse Schade* – a great shame – *Zu viel seelische Anstrengung* – perhaps too much mental excitement?'

'We certainly never get any physical excitement,' I replied, anxious to sign off this unpleasant conversation. 'To what do we owe, seeing you here so early?'

'The Kommandant entered the hospital yesterday with a slight illness. I have come to see him on business and wished to make sure the guard arrangements were adequate.'

'Well, they are,' I said.

After he left, I thought of his remark, 'Too much mental excitement.' What did he mean? Did he know anything? My nerves were jangling, and all morning I was worried. Van Zouco was out. I got hold of Gerda and asked her to find out if the Kommandant really was in hospital. She came back to say that he was and that nearly his whole staff had been to see him during the morning. The more I heard, the more uneasy I became.

When Van Zouco came back from the medical board at lunch

time, he already knew about Haberhauer's visit. He, too, was obviously worried, which I considered to be a good sign as it indicated that he regarded his interests as identified with mine.

'Well,' he said after lunch, 'what we do? You meet him all the same?'

'Yes, as arranged,' I replied, 'but try to find out where Haberhauer is from 2 pm on.' It was all I could do.'

At two o'clock we heard that Haberhauer was nowhere to be seen in the hospital. At two-thirty Van Zouco came to my room, told the guard he was taking me to see a doctor, and we went together down the stairs leading to the church door. Van Zouco was visibly nervous. Now that the moment had arrived, I didn't feel nervous any longer. Just as we entered the chapel and closed the door behind us, I saw Haberhauer leaving the hospital at the far end of the corridor, fifty metres away. Too late to go back now, but I didn't like it.

The church was dead quiet. The gloom was pierced by a few shafts of winter sunlight slanting through the stained glass windows. I felt that sense of awe that Roman Catholic churches often give you. In the back row, in the agreed-upon place, sat the man I supposed we were to meet. He sat there, dressed in a leather overcoat with a camera on a strap around his neck. His face was slightly upturned and illuminated dramatically by one of the beams of sunlight coming through the high nave windows. I looked quickly around the church. Two women were kneeling five rows in front, a soldier was sitting in one of the front seats. Several older people were drifting aimlessly around the aisles; it looked quite normal.

Hearing us enter, the man turned his face slightly. He was about thirty-five, with a good-looking, strongly cut Slav face, and blond hair. After a direct look at me, he turned again to his front.

I went over with Van Zouco, and we knelt down beside him. As I knelt down, he gripped my hand.

'Come back here with me,' he said in German.

Getting up, he moved quickly and quietly to the back of the church and entered a dark, unlit vestibule leading to the organ loft. I followed him with Van Zouco, my heart beating hard.

'I am from the Czech Underground army. I will be glad to tell you anything I can.'

There was no time for lengthy talk about identities. I decided to trust him.

For ten minutes in whispers we talked. As far as he could, he gave me answers to the questions I put to him. First I wanted to know the political composition of the movement. According to him it was pro-British. I asked him where their HQ was and how I could establish contact. He said he would have to ask his chief about that. He told me details of a plan already formulating to take over our camp and free us if it should later come into a German operational back area. He told me the friendliest areas in the Protectorate in which to get help, the best terrain in which to hide large numbers. And then he started to write out, slowly because of the darkness, two addresses in Prague, where help could be found by British officers on the run.

Suddenly, we heard heavy footsteps on the stone floor of the church, and Van Zouco, who had been acting as lookout, moved back farther into the darkness and gripped my arm.

'*Ruhe!* Quiet!' he whispered. 'Don't move!' I flattened myself against the wall as I saw two SS Feldwebels walking straight towards us. Just short of us and outside the open entrance to our little vestibule, they halted. My heart was beating so that it sounded to me like a military drum.

They stood there for at least one minute, motionless, staring straight ahead, apparently at the three of us. Then, suddenly, they turned and moved off into the church. They had been praying at one of the Stations of the Cross above the door.

But now we had to hurry. As soon as I had written down the addresses, I took the Czech's hand to thank him.

'It has been an honour to help British officers,' he said.

When I got back to my room, I memorised the addresses and burned the paper. We had been lucky: Haberhauer had not come to the British ward; apparently all was well. Then Van Zouco came in. He was white as death.

'You know why Haberhauer came here to see the Kommandant? This week the Gestapo shot some British officers who escaped from Stalag Luft III in cold blood. Christ,' he sat down on the bed, 'the murderous bastards.'

This really was bad news, a case so shocking that it was later to figure in the Nürnberg war criminal trials and was one of the few pieces of evidence which thoroughly embarrassed Goering. As later became known, what had happened was murder pure and simple. Each prisoner, on being recaptured, had been handed over to the SS who had shot them out of hand 'attempting to escape'. This was one of the first indications we had of that Nazi brutality which later in the war was to become more evident.

With a guilty conscience such as I had, there was no peace of mind after this.

When I got back to camp that night, I found Mark and David eating supper, both looking very gloomy.

'Peter Griffiths was killed today trying to escape from a train,' David said bluntly.

Apparently, just after I went to Zwittau, Peter Griffiths, one of the special mission, had been ordered to transfer to another camp. He had volunteered to escape from the train and carry out his reconnaissance mission as planned. His jump from the train, executed during a diversion created by two brother officers, had resulted in his death.

This first casualty had the effect one would expect. From those in the camp who disapproved of the large-scale escape plans, there came strong criticism that the point of view adopted by us was too operational and not in conformity with the Geneva Convention. They called Peter's death an unnecessary casualty in aid of a wild scheme. They overlooked the fact that it would have been hard to stop Peter Griffiths from trying to escape – if not in this way, then in another.

These criticisms naturally disturbed David, particularly as we envisaged possible casualties during the big break, and he had talks with the SBO and Anthony Simkins in the next few days to resolve on a way of handling this attitude where it existed in the camp.

But the information I had brought back from Zwittau had

given us just that insight into the situation inside Czechoslovakia which we needed to encourage us in our planning. Points which had perplexed us had been clarified, and certain new possibilities had opened up in view of the new contacts I had made. So that David, backed by the SBO, felt we must push on faster than ever to get the mission out on their reconnaissance. We would waste no time compromising with minority camp opinion, which Anthony Simkins, in any case, handled masterfully. The camp mood continued to be harmonious and solidly behind the escape plan.

Next week, therefore, Ian Howie, tied up and buried under great bundles of the camp's dirty laundry in an act that had been rehearsed for weeks, was carried out of the camp without detection. An unfortunate deviation in the route of the laundry wagon led to his break-out, timed by counting to himself, taking place just when the guards were best placed to cover him. He was chased through the town and eventually cornered in a brickmakers' yard. Fortunately, he got rid of all the compromising documents and letters he was carrying.

Although we had lost two of our best men on the reconnaissance team in Howie, doing thirty days' solitary, and Griffiths killed, we had to get on with organizing escape for the rest of the mission. Our plan was ingenious, and rehearsals for carrying it out had been going on for weeks.

There were two rings of barbed wire around the mile perimeter of the camp. Ten feet of ground in between was used as a lane by sentries going to and fro from their posts. It was also used for conducting Russian prisoners of war to the camp where they worked every day under guard. Entrance from the camp into the lane was by a locked gate in the inner wire. There was another gate about 800 yards away which led through the outer wire into the open country near a farmyard.

Our plan was based on using these two gates, which meant that both locks would have to be picked. To find someone who could do this, Simkins's security officers canvassed the camp to find a lock-picker. Eventually they found one in Lieutenant Curly Lang, whose hobby apparently was lock-picking! For several weeks we sent him around practising his art on every lock in the camp. His instruments were improvised but he kept improving them and eventually was satisfied.

At the same time two German uniforms were being made by our tailors, one for an under officer and one for private. Two more were made up to resemble the ragged green outfits with red patches worn by the Russians.

And so, on Hitler's birthday, 20th April, two Russian POWs carrying shovels and under the guard of a German underofficer and a private walked slowly from behind one of the barracks up to the gate in the inner wire. The underofficer opened the gate with his key, exchanged a few words with the sentry in the tower near by, and took his party into the lane between the inner wire and the outer wire. Walking unhurriedly for nearly a quarter of a mile past all the machine-gun towers, he let himself and his party out by his key at the far gate and disappeared into the farmyard.

The German underofficer was Curly Lang, our lock-picker, and the other guard was Wadeson. Hill and McKenzie were the Russians.

The special mission was away.

David and I had watched the incident with tense faces. But as we saw the little party disappear into the open countryside on the far side of the farmyard, we looked at each other and grinned for the first time in a month. After all the recent disappointments, a first success came as a tonic. The weeks of rehearsal in all details of the ruse, the practice on locks, timing, and the right atmosphere of casualness, all this had made for success.

Each member of the mission had a task. McKenzie and Wadeson were to go to an address in Prague, given me in the church as a principal contact. Their objective was to investigate and report back on areas where we could expect help on the scale we would need. Hill, speaking fluent Czech, carried a lot of money with him, and was to freelance and report back on any new lines he could establish. Lang was free to do as he liked.

All had specific questions to answer, and were to send the answers back through the communication routes established by Howie.

But then, two days later, rumours began to drift in that something

127

had happened in Märisch Trübau. At first these rumours were very vague, and we feared that they had something to do with the mission. By evening, Howie, back from his jail sentence, had the story from his contacts.

On Hitler's birthday, the very day of the break, the Gestapo had discovered plans for the takeover of our immediate area by the Czech resistance. One hundred arrests had been made in Märisch Trübau alone; two of those arrested had hung themselves in the local jail. Coffins in a lunatic asylum had been found stacked with machine guns smuggled in from Poland, and a dynamite charge had been laid to blow up a local factory. Worst of all, they had found a list of 500 names of anti-German elements in the area. They had also found plans for the liberation of our camp exactly as told to me by my contact in the hospital chapel. It was clear that the escape that had just taken place would be related by the Germans to the evidence they had discovered of a planned uprising.

Within twelve hours, our friend the Czech carpenter to whom we owed our wireless was in jail and we never saw him again; we heard that he had been shot.

The three collaborating workers were arrested but released later. The Germans immediately started to fortify the camp for defence against possible attack from outside. Haberhauer's security police, on duty inside the camp, trebled. Every day I saw men from the Gestapo, identifiable by their leather overcoats and black hats, coming and going in the Kommandantur. There was no doubt that the Germans were worried. As a matter of fact, so were we.

The main thing was that McKenzie and Wadeson, the key men for the successful planning of the big break, were still free, although Lang and Hill had been recaptured not far from the camp. Everything now depended on getting the best possible information back so that final plans could be made, based on facts, not surmise.

By this time, as a result of the political situation in Czechoslovakia as described by the Czech agent – also from what we heard on the BBC Czech broadcasts – David had decided to make the main object of the big break a good-will mission to the Protectorate. As prisoners of war we were forbidden by the Geneva Convention to bear arms and, therefore, to join in sabotage and partisan activity within the borders of Germany and its occupied territories. But David conceived that one hundred or more British officers living in Czechoslovakia amongst the people themselves, and identified with their interests, would give an important indication of the West's solidarity with the Czech cause. We thought, that it could even have political results after the war. As it turned out we were correct. The Communist element that forced Beneš out of office after the war fuelled their propaganda with the line that the Western powers had shown little interest in the plight of those Czechs who looked to them for demonstrable support. It was with this object in view that David was by now orienting plans for the June break over the wire.

Those volunteering were all personally interviewed by David. He emphasized that, by signing on for the job, each man surrendered his chances of final escape from German-dominated Europe, as he would be committed to remain in the Protectorate for the duration: that each would run considerable risks for a purpose not immediately obvious and whose long-term value could only be assessed after the war. Of course, the view we had of the situation around us was only a worm's eye view, but at least the objectives were positive.

During that last week in April, German vigilance increased. There was a search somewhere every day, and two more of our best hides were discovered.

Now the Czech propaganda broadcasts from England started up, inciting the Czechs to rise against the Germans, who were in difficulty in Slovakia and Hungary. There was an air of tension among the Germans, unmistakable to the few of us who knew what was going on.

Just then, I was told to be ready to go to Lamsdorf, about 100 miles to the north near Breslau, for final repatriation examination by the Swiss commission. There was much information I could give if I got back to England, particularly regarding the internal situation in Czechoslovakia as we saw it and if I got back to London I could provide liaison for David, if, as he hoped, he succeeded in getting hold of a transmitter once he was free. I made all arrangements for wireless tie-up frequencies, times of calling, etc., before leaving. These were very optimistic plans.

Forty of us went to Lamsdorf and, although some were limbless, and no one was in a fit condition to escape, the Germans sent two officers and a guard of sixty men with us. This provides a good commentary on their attitude towards British prisoners just at that time, and of their fears of what British officers could do in the Protectorate if they got loose.

During my time at Lamsdorf, an enormous British camp for other ranks, I was able to contact the camp leader, RSM Sheriff, of the Royal Welch Fusiliers. He was a Dunkirk prisoner whose performance for five years in the administration, discipline and welfare of the 40,000 other rank prisoners under his command was one of the finest examples of character and leadership shown by any prisoner throughout the war.

He sent his escape representative to see me in the camp hospital. From him I got the address of a prisoner clearing agency in Budapest and one at Metz. He it was, too, who told me that the number of officers shot at Stalag Luft III was around fifty, but he knew no more than this. I failed the repatriation examination, and next day the party returned to Märisch Trübau.

As we marched back to the camp, I saw at once that something was up. Vans of furniture were leaving the camp and the Kommandantur was a hive of activity. I went straight to my room to find David.

'The whole camp is to move,' said David. 'We move out in parties over the next five days. Van Zouco tells me that the new site is near Brunswick and the whole thing is a rush job as they didn't know about it in the Kommandantur until the day before yesterday. A thousand troops have been sent to help in the move and every bloody thing here except the buildings is going. So that's that! I've got everything organized while you've been away. The escape platforms aren't ready yet so the escape is off. All maps, documents, compasses and the wireless are packed in false compartments of packing cases to go with the heavy stuff. The cases have been searched already and nothing was discovered. I'm keeping the number two wireless behind, hidden in a portable gramophone, to give us news for the next five days. You and I will stay behind alone in the compartment of Enterprise X and go to Prague to tell Wadeson and McKenzie what has happened, carrying on as best we can alone. All our necessary documents, Czech passports, money, maps and two suits of civilian clothes are down there waiting for us now. Also food and water for fourteen days.'

Thus David dealt with the winding up of all our activitites of the last four months, transferred the useful part to the new camp and settled our own future. There was no use spending time bemoaning the bad luck. But not many people knew as well as I did how much imagination and organizing talent David had put into the work of those four months, and how bitter the disappointment was to see everything written off by an unpredictable chance.

In those days, we could not decide what had caused the Germans to make this move at such quick notice. From the point of view of resources, men and transport, it was fantastically extravagant. We thought of everything: the Russians approaching in the east, the danger of liberation by Czechs, the grouping of all prisoners of war in central Germany preceding invasion. Later, and certainly after the war, it became clear that after the Stalag Luft III escape and the discoveries on Hitler's birthday, the Gestapo had reached their own conclusions. They must have assumed we were planning a rising in collaboration with the Czech Underground. In any case a rapid decision had clearly been made in Berlin that we were to be at once removed to an area remote from the Protectorate. Added to this, as was later learnt, and written about after the war, activities of subversive elements inside Germany, such as those of Fromm, Goerdeler and Witzleben were becoming known to Hitler. Indeed, all were actively involved in Von Stauffenberg's attempt on his life in the following July.

Van Zouco now told us he had heard that Haberhauer suspected that David and I ran whatever organization existed in the camp. If this was true, he would undoubtedly make sure that we, at least, passed correctly through the identification parade when leaving. So, in order to complicate matters for the Germans, the Senior British Officer gave orders that no one was to give his right name when passing out, and I arranged for four different pairs of officers to say that they were David and I. Also, we immediately moved out of our room, leaving in our places Arthur Gilbey, who slightly resembled David, and Jack Comyn, a brother 8th Hussar of mine, who was to take over from me after my escape. We ourselves went to live in an enormous dormitory in the Biscuit Factory, where we would be hard to find. The chaos in these days of moving was complete, but, even so, David had to stay in his room and indeed in his bunk, as his 6 feet 5 inches were impossible to disguise. I managed to move about and to do what organizing remained, by shaving off my moustache, parting my hair in the middle and plastering it down, and wearing thick-lensed horn-rimmed spectacles. I changed my voice, and the rhythm of my walk and found that people who knew me as well as Jack White Abbott and John Newman didn't recognize me. I met Haberhauer several times without attracting his attention.

Haberhauer knew that there was one project undiscovered because his mine-detecting apparatus had previously registered the noise of digging in the general area of the SBO's quarters. He now started a day and night search for it, supervised by four very astute and specially trained security police. He was apprehensive at the thought of losing prisoners through a last-minute escape. On the third day of the move, when the camp had been nearly emptied and it was getting time for David and I to go into our hiding place, I was looking out the window when I saw Haberhauer running in a state of great excitement out of the SBO's bungalow. I had no doubt as to what had happened and I was right. He had discovered the underground compartment of Enterprise X and all our beautiful equipment.

We did have a second string hide prepared, a large concrete compartment in the roof of one of the buildings where previously we had stored about half a ton of chocolate for the June escape. This had all the necessary escaping equipment as well as food and water, but we had considered the place itself to be more vulnerable to search – mistakenly as it turned out.

But worse was to come. On the morning of the fourth day, David made one of his rare exits from our room to wash and shave in the bathroom. We were walking down the corridor when

Haberhauer appeared suddenly from around the corner. He made a run for David and caught him. I moved on, glasses, buck teeth and parted hair giving me a moment's respite. Within an hour, David was locked up in the Kommandantur and, for the first time in over a year, our partnership had been split. At the time, David's capture seemed to be a gratuitous piece of bad luck following on even worse luck. In the light of later events, however, I should say that if he had not been taken on that day, which stopped our escape, we would have both been recaptured and shot within the next two months.

Colonel Waddilove and I then had to discuss what to do with David gone. I wanted to go to Prague to warn McKenzie and Wadeson and take Alastair Cram with me, but Waddilove asked me not to go, as we imagined David would be sent to another camp and he wanted me to stay on to run the organization at Brunswick. I agreed to do this and decided to send Cram to contact McKenzie and Wadeson instead. Alastair had been lying low for two or three months, studying, but volunteered to do the job as soon as I told him what had happened. To hide up with him, I selected a stout fellow called Gaze, who had personally constructed the hide that was to be used, and who naturally wanted to have a chance to use it.

And so that evening we put the two of them in and sealed the hide. This was Alastair's eighth escape; I knew his form so well, and I had complete confidence that he would get to Prague if anyone could. Next morning, as I marched down to the station, nearly the last one to leave, I looked back at the deserted camp and particularly at the hide where Alastair and Gaze were by now installed. I wished them luck with all my heart, but I cannot say that I was not envious.

On reaching the station, an interpreter read out a typically dishonest manifesto from the German High Command, saying that, as the British had repeatedly handcuffed German POWs it was necessary, for reasons of reciprocity, to do the same to us. Our boots and braces were also taken from us, and then into each cattle truck eighteen officers were bundled. They went into one third of the available space, partitioned to the ceiling with barbed wire. We were too confined to lie down. In the other two thirds of the carriage eighteen guards with sub-machine guns tried not to look foolish. Certainly the Herrenvolk were not taking any chances.

Half an hour after the train rattled out, everyone had taken off their handcuffs by opening the locks with jack-knives and had deposited them in the lavatory buckets. When these were full (not only of handcuffs) we got the Germans to empty them out of open car doors. The handcuffs, of course, went too with all the liquid.

Thus, in a small but effectively Rabelaisian way, we paid them back for the discomfort of that two-day trip.

But there was no doubt that they had beaten us over the escape, and there were bitter thoughts in my mind as we travelled along the Elbe through Czechoslovakia that May night, on our way to Brunswick, site of our new camp.

CHAPTER EIGHT

Brunswick and Colditz

When we arrived at Brunswick I saw David getting out of another cattle truck. He had been brought separately under a special guard. I was amazed to see him. The Germans knew every well of our proven capabilities for making trouble, and the prudent thing to do would have been to separate us. But for some reason, they did not.

We settled into yet another camp, this time a former Luftwaffe barrack consisting of four large buildings. The SBO arranged for us to have a room to ourselves in the camp hospital, a small room not more than fifteen feet by eight feet. On the wall, in large black Gothic print was inscribed: '*Ich habe das Reich mit Blut und Eisern verschaffen und ich werde es verteidigen gegen jedermann – Hitler.*'

Thus every day when we woke up we were reminded that Hitler had shaped Germany with blood and iron and would defend it against all comers. In the end we found some paint and got rid of this depressing slogan.

Mark Ogilvie Grant said he would like to pack it in as our backroom boy, and we certainly couldn't blame him. Our clandestine activities meant that there was a constant stream of visitors to our room and no peace at all for him. Arthur Gilbey, a 4th Hussar, volunteered to take his place.

We were lucky to have him. He was a person of great charm and, even more important, possessed of a tolerant nature. He was also a good cook.

By now David had started to think about the war in Japan, and the role his SAS Regiment could play when, as we now hoped, the war in Europe would soon be over. We got hold of maps of

135

China, and, from news in the German papers, started to form a picture of what was happening with Slim's Burma Army and Stilwell's American Force operating with Chiang Kai-shek. David had even contrived a rough plan as to how the SAS should be used in the Far East theatre. He liked thinking ahead, and we had very little else to think about constructively in those days.

We kept wondering what had happened to Wadeson and McKenzie, our special mission, and to Cram, who had volunteered to find them at our Prague contact address. As it was a month since we had heard anything, we assumed that somehow they must have linked up. We were to get a nasty shock.

About three weeks after our arrival, just as we had settled in, the SBO was summoned to the office of the Kommandant. There he was bluntly informed that Wadeson and Mackenzie had been recaptured in Prague and shot while attempting to escape. He presented the SBO with two small lead caskets containing their ashes, and asked, with evident embarrassment, if they should be handed over to the Red Cross.

The story was of course untrue. As was becoming well known, the phrase 'shot while attempting to escape' was a cover-up story of the Wehrmacht. As regular soldiers, it was a source of embarrassment to them that the SS or the Gestapo carried out these murders whenever British officers got outside their control. Execution of prisoners of war was not *ehrlich* – not honourable – under their code. Moreover the Wehrmacht High Command were concerned that they might be held responsible for these murders when the war was over – and the end looked increasingly imminent.

A short time later Alastair Cram arrived, looking a ghost of his former self. He was thin, hollow-eyed and nervous. Apparently after leaving his hiding place at Märisch Trübau he had succeeded in making his way to Prague as planned, walking much of the way. Arriving in Prague he had made contact in a small bar with a Czech who professed to be anti-Nazi and who volunteered to introduce Alastair to a safe house. The safe house proved to belong to the Gestapo. As he was dressed in good civilian clothes and had in his possession Clayton's forged identity papers, ration cards and money. The Gestapo arrested him at once. He was imprisoned in the Gestapo jail, the old Hradćany Palace, and given a rough time under interrogation. In view of what had happened to Wadeson and McKenzie, it was a miracle that he had been released and sent back to us. I knew Alastair pretty well and I could see that he was shaken.

These events were very disturbing, and it worried David and me to think of our responsibility for sending these three volunteers on a task that had turned out so tragically. We were soon to have something more personal to worry about.

Van Zouco went out regularly to the Kommandantur, ostensibly on hospital business. This was useful as he brought back bits of gossip from time to time.

One day he came into our room, clearly agitated. I was alone.

'My best fellow,' he said to me nervously, 'there is some bad news for you!'

'We've had enough bad news. What is it now?'

He stammered out his story. When he was excited his English was never good.

'I hear from the Germans that you and Stirling are tried when you are not there by a criminal court because you are enemies of the Reich.' (Why not, I thought.) 'You have been *Zum Tod beurteilt*' (sentenced to death – he didn't know the English for it). 'They don't tell you this. But if you act something more against them, they do this immediately!'

This was bad news. From now on we would be sitting ducks; and we were clearly in deeper trouble than we had thought we were. Looking back years later, I believe that this sentence was not passed at all, but that the Germans had given the news to Van Zouco knowing he would pass it on to us and that it might temper our activities. It would be improbable that the SBO would not have been officially informed of the sentence. But at the time we were not so rational about it and we didn't sleep well that night.

*

Events of a more important nature were about to happen, events that boosted the camp's morale. It was June 1944 and the invasion of

Europe took place. Within two months our armies were heading for Paris and Brussels. And in late July, Count von Stauffenberg, a colonel on Hitler's staff, made an attempt on the Führer's life at his Prussian headquarters. It was unsuccessful, but the idea that there existed a German resistance movement cheered us all up. David and I regained our good spirits and optimism.

Then one day in August while we were sitting in our room talking about what we would do after the war, the SBO came in. He looked very serious.

'The Kommandant has just given me the order that you are both to be at the prison gate in one hour with all your belongings. I asked him where you were going, but he said he didn't know. An outside officer will conduct you. That was all he would say.'

I must admit that my knees buckled as I heard this news. It sounded ominously as if we were being set up to be 'shot while escaping'.

Knowing the Wehrmacht's traditional respect for the officer class, David and I now put on battle-dress, rank badges and medals, hoping in this way to underline our rights as regular soldiers under the Geneva Convention. The SBO told the Kommandant that he would be held personally responsible if anything happened to us. Then we went to the gate and were escorted out. We were given a wheelbarrow to carry our belongings, and trundled it with our guards towards the city of Brunswick. The camp was on the outskirts. On the way American planes came over and bombed the area heavily. We took refuge until it was over, but we were acutely conscious of the fact that it would now be easy to get rid of us by saying that we had been killed in a bombing raid. The timing was perfect for such a story.

Nevertheless we arrived safe and sound at the Brunswick railway station and boarded a train going east. In due course we arrived at Magdeburg where we boarded another train going south. The guards still wouldn't divulge our destination, but as the train moved from the industrialized north into more rural surroundings we began to feel somewhat reassured. A Gestapo jail was hardly likely to be placed in the middle of farming land, or so we reasoned. Eventually we stopped at a small station,

Colditz. Colditz was in Saxony between Leipzig and Dresden.

'*Aufsteigen,*' said the guard. We got out with our kit.

A great deal has been written about Colditz, which achieved post-war fame as the German *Straflager* or Punishment Camp for prisoners of war. Colditz Castle was on a great rock overlooking the Mulde River and dated back to 1028. It had served many purposes under the Holy Roman Emperors and more latterly under the Electors of Saxony. Like many fortresses it had secret passages and escape routes for use during sieges. During its five years as a prisoner of war camp there had been dozens of escape attempts, and by the time we arrived the Germans had it completely sealed up.

This, then, was the castle we looked at as we were marched from the station up the hill to its gates. The approach was almost identical with that of Gavi in Italy – both sited in mediaeval times as fortresses and defensive strong points. Crossing over a moat, we entered the castle keep through a huge archway and were met by the Security Officer, Hauptmann Egger, who supervised our search in a small cell. Then we were led up a ramp where iron doors opened allowing us to enter a courtyard about forty yards square bounded on all four sides by the castle buildings. This turned out to be the only exercise space for the 350 inmates.

It was a warm day in late August 1944. All around the courtyard offers were sitting, backs to the wall, sunning themselves, chatting or reading. Martin Gilliat, adjutant to Colonel Willie Tod, the SBO, met us. At the same time a dozen other officers whom we already knew came across to greet us. It was a friendly arrival and, for once, David and I felt almost happy to be locked up safely – safe, that is, from the risk of being shot while attempting to escape.

Gilliat took us up two flights of narrow stone stairs inside a turret. At the top we came to a corridor and at the end of it we entered a room which was to be our quarters and our mess. Feeding arrangements at Colditz were such that half a dozen officers ate together, with basic food provided by the central kitchen, anything more being the affair of the mess itself.

We were fortunate in our new companions, to whom Gilliat

introduced us. One was Peter Dollar, a 4th Hussar captured in Greece whom I knew from pre-war days as a polo player of international class. There was Douglas Bader, the famous legless RAF pilot, and our elder statesman, Colonel 'Daddy' Stayner of the Dorset Regiment who was also our cook. 'Daddy' Stayner had been at Colditz a long time and had been SBO during troubled times. Tall, silver haired and handsome, he was cool and imperturbable.

Douglas Bader provided the fun. He was fanatically anti-German, and baited them at every possible opportunity. The Germans, who respected his courage, gave him privileges and let him get away with things that would otherwise be forbidden or punishable. Most important, they allowed him one hot bath a week which he shared with the rest of the mess. We were the envy of the castle. They also allowed him to go for a two-hour walk in the countryside twice a week so that he could exercise muscles at the top of his thighs which he needed to propel his two aluminium legs. Peter Dollar was allowed to go with him. When he went out, although he had two guards with him, he openly traded the contents of our Red Cross parcels with local farmers who gave him barley in return. This provided much-needed bulk food in that last winter of the war. The grain he brought back in sacks which he hung from his waist inside his trouser legs, and it was distributed throughout the castle to be made into porridge. It was hard work for Douglas, walking up the steep hill to the castle with thirty pounds of grain hanging from his legs, but he laughed it off as a great joke.

Such behaviour was simply out of the question for a normal prisoner. It was also out of the question for a guard to permit contact with the local populace, not to say trade with them. But Douglas tamed his guards and got away with it; and in that last winter of the war we were very grateful for the supplement to our diet that he provided.

He had another ruse which he used against the Germans. If they wanted to see him, for whatever reasons, he always asked them to come to our room. There he would greet them propped up in his bunk, a truncated body, with his aluminium legs on the bed beside him. He found that this kind of reception embarrassed the Germans and made it impossible for them effectively to discipline him or get him to agree to anything. He would wave one of his legs at the German, much as a school teacher would wave a pencil at a pupil, and address them in a language that would put anyone else in solitary for a month. Douglas enjoyed every minute of these encounters, and Peter Dollar was a constant and willing partner in this baiting.

We settled in quickly with our new messing companions and now, for the first time since capture, I put escape out of my mind. This was because the Germans had issued an order that any prisoner attempting to escape would be shot. In all fairness it was hard to complain about this, although it was quite contrary to the Geneva Convention. The simple fact was that after the Normandy invasion the Germans not only feared uprisings by European Resistance movements but also mass uprisings by prisoners of war. Some camps were very big. The one for other ranks that I had seen at Lamsdorf held 30,000 prisoners. And so I settled down to do some serious reading, just waiting for the end. We felt sure that by now it would not be much longer.

I punctuated my studies by walking around the castle, visiting other rooms, gossiping with old acquaintances and making some new ones. My impressions made it possible to compare the two special camps – Colditz in Germany and Gavi in Italy. Only Stirling and I had been in both of them.

The principal resemblance between the two lay in their exceptional morale. This morale derived from the calibre of the officers – all men of adventurous character and possessed of optimistic initiative. There the likeness stopped.

Colditz opened its mediaeval gates to prisoners in 1940, and during the next five years developed an esprit de corps resembling that of a good regiment. For much of this time British officers were in a majority, but the prison from time to time also harboured Poles, French, Dutch and Americans, which gave it an international flavour. The Allied fortunes had sometimes been pretty gloomy, especially until 1943; but I don't think there had been a day when anyone doubted the outcome, or let up on the war in microcosm that was waged inside the castle walls.

The files of Colditz prisoners were labelled '*Deutschfeindlich*' – hostile to Germany – and this title was richly deserved.

Gavi, on the other hand, only existed for eighteen months in all, that is from early 1942 until the Italian capitulation in September 1943. Nevertheless, during this short length of time it had developed a character of its own. Unlike the European mixture of officers in Colditz, Gavi was a prison of Commonwealth officers – British, South African, Australian, and New Zealanders. Their solidarity was based on having a common background; the Middle East campaigns.

Colditz prisoners were in a way institutionalized. By that I meant that they had had time – in some cases five years – in which to settle into established routines. Days were carefully marked out into periods for study, listening to lectures, rehearsing amateur dramatics, playing netball, domestic duties for the mess, or, in previous years, planning escapes. There was an excellent library with a wide variety of books.

Gavi was short of books and had no radio. The population was fairly transient. As a result, life was more extrovert. Officers walked up and down the ramp or in the courtyard planning what they would do when Italy was forced out of the war. In the evening they met to drink a ration of marsala. At night rooms became casinos with Faro and Blackjack. Only one escape took place during the months it served as a prison. It was, as I have recounted, a fortress with virtually no exits.

And then methods of guarding prisoners was quite different in the two places. At Gavi, guards were posted not only around the outside of the fortress, but also at many strategic points inside. Carabinieri strolled through the living quarters at all times of the day and night. They would look under the occasional mattress, empty a tin of margarine to see if it hid anything, search through the pockets of a coat hanging on the wall, or simply stand for half a hour at a time, gazing at the life going on around them.

At Colditz, except at night and during roll calls, no guards entered the castle. Even officers were limited to Hauptmann Eggers, in charge of security, and Hauptmann Püpcke, who took roll calls. The guarding was all outside, but there was plenty of it.

*

Autumn and winter passed quickly. The news was good and we heard it all on our secret radio.

In January Hitler's last offensive in the Ardennes was crushed. The Russians were making enormous advances on the Eastern Front, and by March had overrun East Prussia, Poland and Silesia. In February from our windows we saw the sky lit up thirty miles to the east by the devastating Allied bombing of Dresden. In the west, the Rhine was crossed, and the Allied armies moved on a wide front into Germany. By early April it was clear that the last days of Hitler's Third Reich were at hand and that we would soon be free. Or that is how it appeared. But it was not quite as simple as that.

Early in that last winter of the war, Colonel Willie Tod, the SBO, was informed that the camp had been removed from control of the Wehrmacht and was to come under Himmler, although SS troops did not actually take over guard duties. This was a worrying development, as we in Germany were well aware what it meant to come under orders from this brutal man. Moreover, we had heard through the grapevine that Colditz prisoners might he held as hostages at the end of the war, and especially a group in the camp whom the Germans called *Prominenten*.

Prominenten were officers whose families in one way or another were important. Michael Alexander was related to the Field Marshal. The Master of Elphinstone was a kinsman of the Queen, as was Lord Lascelles. Lord Hopetoun's father had been Viceroy of India; Lord Haig was the son of the Field Marshal; Giles Romilly was related to Churchill; John Winant's father was the American Ambassador in London. Early in the year these officers were put together under special guard in cells off the courtyard. When the commander of the Warsaw Underground, General Bor Komorowski arrived in February, he joined them with three of his generals.

Other worrying rumours started to circulate. It was planned, so we heard, that in the last resort Hitler, with his most fanatical supporters and an élite army of the SS, would withdraw to what came to be called the National Redoubt, above Salzburg in the Alps. There they would fight to the bitter end, and Hitler would bring hostages from all the enemy territories with him, including the prisoners of Colditz.

This was probably Goebbels's idea. General Omar Bradley wrote in his biography that Eisenhower took the information so seriously that it influenced tactical movements of his armies right up to the end. This idea – a Goebbels and Hitler fantasy – was described by Keitel, Chief of the German General Staff, during the Nuremberg trials as 'mostly nonsense'.

And so the atmosphere in the camp was decidedly uneasy. In February Colonel Tod decided to take action. He was a Scots Fusilier captured at Dunkirk and a man of great character whom the Germans not only respected but feared because of the loyalty he commanded from those under him. He reckoned, with the Allies approaching from the west and the Russians from the east, that we might be caught in between and have to fend for ourselves. In that case we would need links with locals in authority and to establish a workable relationship with them before a dangerous situation actually arose. To be practical we would have to make these contacts immediately, and work on them so that they would be ready to accept directions from us when the country started to fall apart, as we were sure it would.

Colonel Tod knew of David Stirling's Märisch Trübau project which had been oriented more or less along these same lines and for the same reasons. Now he enlisted David to apply the same concept to the Colditz problem.

Could such a thing be done? Colonel Tod asked. In spite of natural optimism and a tendency to take on anything that seemed difficult, David's answer had to be 'possibly', but 'probably not'. For prisoners in the closest-guarded prison in Germany to develop contacts with dissident Germans outside seemed out of the question, even with the war clearly in its closing stages.

We talked about it. There was one first step that was feasible. All individual trading with guards could be stopped. As

144

happened in all prisons, quite a few officers developed a relationship with their own pet guards, and they would trade with them when they came in at night in return for gossip from the Kommandantur, and luxuries such as schnapps and bread. But we needed a specific kind of information, not just gossip. This meant we would have to forbid general trading and keep it strictly in our hands. Once this was done, we could appoint traders who would operate under our instructions and ask only those questions directly related to the task the SBO had set us.

The SBO immediately gave the order for trading to stop, and placed at David's disposal the reserve of Red Cross parcels that he had set aside for emergencies.

Resistance to this idea by those whose blackmarket supplies had been cut off, was overcome by arranging for a general distribution throughout the castle of all produce procured through controlled trading. So far so good.

Now the important thing was to put together a team capable of suborning the guards, men with a talent for persuasion and some flair for intelligence work. It was my job to do this, but I needed a professional to help me.

This was to be Pierre de Vomécourt whom David and I had got to know well since coming to Colditz. His story was interesting. Pierre was a Frenchman, educated in England, and bilingual. He was one of the first to leave France after the Armistice in 1940, signing up with SOE, who were recruiting volunteers for the Resistance, to return to France. While operating there with a team of four he was betrayed by the notorious turncoat French woman agent known as 'La Chatte' and sent to Fresnes prison in Paris. For two years he faced repeated sessions of inter-rogation at the Gestapo headquarters in the Avenue Foch. These interrogations had the aim of making him admit he was an agent of SOE, and to learn about their activities, but more important to make him give away his contacts. He denied knowledge of SOE, never gave away anyone, and never altered his story. In the end the Gestapo gave up, awarded him the officer status he claimed and sent him with his team to Colditz. David and I both recognized his sharp intelligence and steely nerves, and these were coupled with a talent for deception. He was an ideal partner.

With Pierre I now set about choosing two officers who would be our contacts with the Germans and who would have sole call on our store of cigarettes, chocolate and gold.

Our first choice was Lieutenant Cenek Chaloupka, a Czech Air Force officer who had successively flown for Czechoslovakia, Poland, France and England – and had been decorated by all four countries. 'Cheko', as he was called, was a strikingly good-looking man of about thirty, tall and swarthy with a charismatic character, and possessed of an irresistible exuberance. He spoke perfect German, and already had his special friends among the guards. Above all, he was a man of complete discretion and of proven courage.

Dick Jones was our other choice. To this day I do not know what his real name was, nor his real nationality, although I suspect it was Egyptian. Dick turned up at Colditz claiming a varied career as a spy for the British; claims which he supported with stories about his work in French-occupied North Africa, latterly in Tunis. These tales made him suspect in the castle, as spies do not as a rule talk about their work. His presence in Colditz therefore had been viewed with a certain jaundiced reserve, which was reinforced by the fact that he spoke practically no English, but fluent French, German, Italian and Arabic. Dick's manner was bland and his personality grey. He was eminently forgettable, exactly what an agent should be.

If what he said about himself was true, he could be useful to us. But dare we trust him? It so happened, however, that David had heard of his exploits when in Tunis. We talked this over and finally decided to treat him as we had treated Van Zouco at Märisch Trübau, that is, to use him, but to tell him nothing. As it turned out, we had made an excellent choice: Dick proved to be a courageous and loyal partner in our project.

These two, then, had the task of obtaining information in return for bribes of chocolate and cigarettes, and of trying through the guards to make some contact with locals in Colditz town. At this stage the guards were men of over sixty and there were a few young boys of about sixteen. This worked in our favour as there was not much zeal for the war in either of these age groups, and they were susceptible to the Allied propaganda that Cheko and Dick put out with great skill.

Both Cheko and Dick had a lot of experience in trading with the guards. They knew the 'going rate' – just how much information to ask for, how much to offer in exchange in order to coax out more, when to shut off supplies, when to be amiable, when to be tough. Every night they met their contacts, guards who came into the courtyard from 6 pm until 6 am, standing, one just inside each of the five entrances to our quarters, forbidding us free movement. There were no guards inside the castle during the day, but the night routine provided an excellent opportunity for cosy chats, although it was necessary to wait for tame guards to come on duty. This often meant waiting around all night inside the doorway as the guard rosters were somewhat unpredictable.

During these talks Cheko and Dick questioned the guards along lines laid down by Pierre, David and myself, lines calculated to give us precise information about the important personalities in Colditz, and the activities in the German Camp Kommandantur. We also looked for information as to the location of the police station, the mayor's office, the telephone exchange, waterworks, the concentration camp for Hungarian Jews, barracks of Russian prisoners of war, grain and petrol stores, garages, medical facilities and main farm buildings. We had rapid success in obtaining this information, and soon had a map of Colditz with all key points accurately marked, aided in this by the fact that from the castle we had a panoramic view of the village below and could relate what we heard from the guards to what we could actually see. David passed on this information to the SBO as it came in.

But our prime object was to find and develop one reliable anti-Nazi contact in the village. We were despairing of this until we had an unusual piece of luck. I discovered that Cheko, dashing officer that he was, had a girl friend in the village.

'What do you mean?' I asked him when he told me this. 'How can you have any friend in the village?'

'It happened last year. I was sent to Prague for interrogation by the Gestapo. There was a girl from Colditz in the same carriage, a dentist's assistant. It was quite a long trip and we had time to get to know each other a bit. I thought I would never come back from Prague – I had a guilty conscience. But I did, in three days' time.'

When he got out of the train, the girl, Imgard Wernicke, was on the platform to meet him.

'I've met every train from Prague hoping you would come back. Thank God you have.'

Cheko asked the guard to give him a minute alone with the girl. He agreed, backing off into a corner but keeping watch.

'No one knows what is going to happen to Germany now. And the castle is a dangerous place for all of you. I want to see you again. Can't you get to the dentist somehow? I want to see you again,' she repeated.

Cheko said he would try – after all, Colditz prisoners were short of female companionship and this was a chance in a thousand.

Cheko had managed to get to the dentist, not once but five times, by smashing a few teeth so badly on rocks that they needed a series of treatments.

Each time he managed to see Imgard alone. Indeed he became the only inmate of the castle ever to have kissed a girl while being held there.

On the last visit she told him that she would do anything for him, and to contact her through a guard if he ever needed help.

When we heard this the next step was obvious. Somehow we had to find a guard whom we could trust to carry a letter to Imgard, as she was our one chance of making contact with people of the town. It was a delicate task. At first neither Cheko nor Dick Jones admitted to knowing a guard who they were prepared to trust with this sort of mission.

Then one day Dick Jones came to us. As usual he had the faintest of smiles on his face, but his eyes never smiled.

'There is a new guard,' he said. 'Only a boy really, but he said he would buy things for us in the village if we gave him the

money. His family live in Colditz,' he added. I asked Pierre de
Vomécourt what he thought.

'If he is prepared to take that kind of risk,' Pierre said, 'he
might carry a letter, especially if we can convince him that he is
only helping a romance.'

We brought Cheko in at this point, and got him to write a
romantic letter to Imgard. We left the envelope open. The boy,
Heinz by name, readily agreed to deliver it, and to bring back the
reply, which he did. This was progress; and after a few exchanges
we sealed all envelopes and got down to business.

After the necessary fond preludes, the letters turned into
questionnaires, and were in fact, written by Pierre and myself for
Cheko to copy. The questions dealt with subjects of national
interest: morale, attitudes towards the Allies, and towards the
Nazi party, but more especially with the situation in Colditz and
its surroundings. Who were the leading Nazis? Were there any
anti-Nazis?

She answered these questions carefully and intelligently. Then,
in one letter came a surprise. Her father was the leader of the local
Nazi Party, and through this connection she had access to
information regarding important Colditz personalities and their
intentions. She was ready, she said, to tell us everything she
could, getting her information directly from her father and
passing it on. She heard a lot of talk between her father and his
Nazi colleagues when they met at her house. Two questionnaires
a week now went out to Imgard and she answered them
thoughtfully and in detail.

We also made progress with Heinz, our courier. Before being
conscripted he had been studying to enter the School of Mines at
Freiberg, and was alert and intelligent. It became obvious that he
was helping us because he was anti-Nazi. We learnt from him
that his father, whom I shall call Schmidt, was the town's richest
man and leading moderate. Schmidt had actually said to him at
the time of the attempt on Hitler's life in July that if he couldn't
be got rid of that way, then somehow another way had to be
found. This was clearly a good subject for us to concentrate on.

The first and riskiest step was to induce Heinz to confide in his father that he was collaborating with us. This he did, and to our surprise got the answer that he was ready to help. Before we asked anything of him, however, we checked with Imgard to find out if he was the moderate his son had made him out to be. The answer came back that he was, and, moreover, was on her father's blacklist.

It was easy now for us to get Imgard to approach Schmidt and to team up with him in helping us. This was done through Cheko's letters and they carried very careful instructions and many questions. Imgard's infatuation with Cheko was complete, and she never hesitated to do as she was told. Very soon, we had a dossier on all the important local Nazis, not only civilians in the Party, but Gestapo and castle administrative personnel. On the other hand we knew who the moderates were in whom Schmidt had confidence. From among the latter on Schmidt's recommendation we selected those whom we would look to with a view to forming an alternative local government when the end came.

Heinz's father now started to prove his usefulness. He somehow arranged that the Kommandantur switchboard operator would listen in on all calls from Berlin and Dresden to the Kommandant. Authorities responsible for Colditz had their headquarters in the two cities. The operator noted the gist of these conversations and in due course we received the information. None of it was reassuring as more and more often the calls came from SS and Gestapo sources. It was also arranged that office staff watched incoming mail for anything affecting our safety. Thus in March, we learnt of an especially disturbing piece of information: a letter had been seen on the Kommandant's desk signed by Hitler saying that the *Prominenten* were under no condition to be allowed to fall into Allied hands. It is of some interest to note that after the war Lord Lascelles (by then Harewood) actually had sight of this order, and it stands as proof of the genuineness of these contacts.

We learnt from the same source that a high official in the German Foreign Office would be arriving to talk to General Bor Komorowski, Commander of the Warsaw Home Army, that army that had risen in Warsaw against the Germans and had been annihilated. I warned him of this, and sure enough, a week later when I was exercising in the courtyard with the General, the security officer came into the yard with two guards and took him out of the castle. I reported this immediately to Colonel Tod. Bor Komorowski would be a prize hostage for the Germans, and, as I continued my walk around the courtyard, my thoughts were apprehensive and pessimistic. I did not expect to see him again.

Half an hour later, to my great surprise, he was released back into the courtyard to join me. The General was a small insignificant-looking man but with a lion's personality. The lion growled.

'*Ils sont fous*,' he said. He spoke no English. 'They offered me my freedom and freedom for all Polish prisoners as well, if I would organize them into a resistance unit that would support Hitler and go underground to continue the war against the Russians. I could have first priority on any arms and supplies I might need.'

'What did you tell them?' I asked.

'I told them no,' he said abruptly. He then went on to talk about other things.

He asked me if I would take back to England his war diary and account of the Warsaw uprising if anything happened to him. The British, he said, had no firsthand details of the struggle that the people of Warsaw and the Home Army had put up, as the only survivors were all prisoners.

From his diary I learnt then what is now well known. The General had calculated that aside from harassing activities of assassination and sabotage, he would only have one chance for a full-scale rising and that would be when either the Russians or the Allies had approached close enough to give aid.

At last, in the early summer of 1944, the Poles in Warsaw sighted Russian tanks on the eastern side of the Vistula. Bor judged this to be the moment and gave the order for Warsaw to rise, at the same time radioing London and Moscow to give all support. What happened was disastrous. The Russians withdrew their tanks, and made no attempt to support the uprising. For whatever reason, we on our side never gave air support that the Poles so badly needed. As a result the Warsaw uprising was put down by the Germans in September 1944 with huge casualties, both military and civilian. Warsaw virtually ceased to exist. It was one of the most courageous, and, as it turned out, one of the most futile actions of the war, as a year later Poland became a satellite of Russia, much of her territory portioned out to Russia.

In April 1945, after I arrived back in England, I delivered Bor's memorandum to the Foreign Office as his whereabouts was still unknown. I have never seen a publication of it, but I have a strong suspicion that it might not reflect well on the actions of the British Government. They, after all, were in those days more interested in avoiding friction with their powerful ally than in helping the country on whose behalf they had gone to war. It is a mark of the General's loyalty that I never heard him express any bitterness about this tragic affair in the years after the war.

But now it was late March, and the war was clearly into its last weeks if not days. Whatever was going to happen to us would happen soon.

We learnt that any orders that could affect us, such as our liquidation or removal as hostages, would come down from Berlin to the Kommandant through the Gauleiter of Saxony whose headquarers were in Dresden. David thought we should threaten him.

Pierre and I drafted a letter couched in menacing tones. It began '*Ihr Tag der Macht ist vorbei. Jetzt stehen Sie den Tod gegenüber*' – your day of power is over. Now you face death. It went on to say that if any harm came to prisoners in Colditz or to prisoners in Saxony at large, the Allies would see to it that he was hung. This letter purporting to come from liberal and Communist elements hostile to the Nazis was translated into idiomatic German by Lance Pope, bilingual and actually married to a German. It was written in Gothic script, and posted in Dresden by Heinz. We hoped it might give the Gauleiter some worried moments, and perhaps make him think twice in a crisis. Of course these activities were known only to the SBO and those concerned.

The last days of Colditz, leading up to its liberation by the Americans, have been vividly described in detail by Pat Reid in his definitive book *Colditz, The Full Story*. Here I am concerned only with how they were related to our small subversive organization. What happened was that by late March we faced the distinct possibility of being squeezed by Patton's advance from the west, and the Russian advance from the east. A dogfight in our immediate area between the Germans and the Russians on one side and the Americans on the other would place us in a dangerous position. It became important therefore for us to have immediate information from our Colditz contacts as to what was going on day by day. We would see German troops moving through Colditz and along the Mulde River below. To be useful, information would have to reach us at once. We could not wait for meetings with Heinz, which could only take place every other night when he came on guard.

It was Colonel Tod's anticipation of just such a situation that had led him to enlist David's help. Now it paid off.

We set up an early warning system. This involved the appointment by Heinz's father of a Colditz man who would be available to give signals which we in the castle could see. This man took up station every day at 9 am, noon, and 4 pm at a lamp post which was visible from the castle on a street at the foot of the hill three hundred feet below us. His movements could be interpreted by us according to a code, and there were four alternative messages that he could give. The first was 'Nothing to report;' the second 'You are to be moved'; the third 'German troops are pulling out' and the fourth 'Break out at all costs.' He could convey one or other of these messages by his actions. Leaning on the lamp post meant one thing; crossing the road another; lighting a cigarette another; and entering the shop behind him gave the danger signal to break out. During the first weeks in early April, Pierre or myself watched at every appointed hour. Until 14th April the signal every day was 'Nothing to report.' And then on that day we got the signal, 'You are to be moved.'

We warned the SBO; and sure enough that day he was

summoned to the Kommandant's office where he was told that everyone was to move at once to the east, that is towards the Russian front. Because of our warning he had had several hours to think about the implications of this, and his answer was immediate: We refuse to move. The Kommandant gave in after long and difficult negotiations by telephone with the General Kommando and we stayed put.

The final act was now about to take place. Our first warning of extreme action had come with the move of the *Prominenten* to Königstein as hostages on 12th April in the middle of the night, an ominous event. Now, with the rapidly deteriorating situation on the German side, the SBO took the initiative and demanded that the castle be handed over to him. This was done, and a formal surrender document was signed with the German Kommandant, although for form's sake the sentries remained at their posts albeit with unloaded arms.

From the castle we had a grandstand view of the final battle about to take place and every window was crammed with spectators. The local German commander reinforced his troops in order to hold the Mulde river crossing at Colditz. These troops were there to oppose the attack coming from the 273rd US Infantry whose advance points were now in woods two miles away at the top of rising ground which we could see. Our fear was that the Americans would put their artillery fire down on the castle, as it would logically be a strong point for German resistance. As it turned out the US heavy artillery had been ordered not to fire on the castle; but nearby American tanks, probing the river crossing, ranged their guns without warning on us. Shots hit the castle and the Kommandantur, but most of them were aimed at the lower walls which were thick enough to withstand their fire. We hung white cloths out of the windows and the firing ceased. At the same time fighting at the bridge petered out as the Germans withdrew. A little later we saw a sergeant and three men of the 273rd Regiment climb the hill to the castle to receive the surrender of the garrison. The gates opened and we were free.

The SBO ordered that we were not to leave the castle as the area around us was still being fought over. However, as we had been responsible for pinpointing essential services, David got permission for us to go and live in Colditz. There we would be able to help the Americans organize the town, and liaise with the moderate Germans. Of course we saw to it that those who had collaborated with us got special treatment and were appointed to key posts; but it was too dangerous for them to be seen associating with us, so that we never met any of them. Our map, pinpointing key points and essential services, saved the Americans a lot of time.

And so, for three days, we lived in luxury in a large house on the river, looked after by a cook and a maid. Heinz's father saw to it that we were supplied with the best of blackmarket rations. Peter Dollar got permission to come and live with us and somehow got hold of a large Mercedes limousine and petrol. We drove around the town in this car. It was more comfortable than the Americans' jeeps and more impressive too. Every night we went around to the compound of some Russian POWs for a party. They had cases of schnapps and a balalaika that accompanied the deafening choruses that went on all night. It was different from castle life to say the least.

We were still in the most forward area of the American advance, and there were roving bands of German soldiers in the nearby forests. For this reason, it had been considered dangerous to transport us through these forests to the rear. However, after three days six American lorries appeared and with one armoured car as escort we were driven back forty miles to a landing strip. It was close to Leipzig; so close; in fact, that artillery was firing not far away.

Four Lancasters were waiting for us. We piled in and a few hours later landed in England.

On our way to the reception centre where we were to be de-briefed, David and I were sitting on the back of an open lorry, legs dangling over the back. The coutryside on that sunny April day was at its best. Some farm labourers working in the fields waved at us.

My reaction was automatic.

'The natives look friendly,' I remarked to David.

It took a few seconds for me to realize that they really were friendly, and that at last there was no need to think of escape. It was going to be quite a change.

Index

Index